BUILDING AND DETAILING

SCALE MODEL
STOCK CARS

BILL COULTER

KALMBACH
BOOKS

Printed in the United States of America

98 99 00 01 02 03 04 05 06 07   10 9 8 7 6 5 4 3 2 1

For more information, visit our website at
http://www.kalmbach.com

Publisher's Cataloging-in-Publication
(Provided by Quality Books, Inc.)

Coulter, Bill.
    Building and detailing scale model stock cars / Bill Coulter. —
1st ed.
    p. cm.
    Includes bibliographical references.
    ISBN: 0-89024-285-2

    1. Automobiles—Models—Design and construction.   I. Title.

TL237.C68 1998   629.22'1
                                      QBI97-41375

Book and cover design: Kristi Ludwig

On the cover: Large picture, 1966 T-Bird, model by Tom Dill. Bottom row (left to right), 1956 Chevy convertible, model by Drew Hierwarter; 1970 Plymouth Superbird, model by Tom Dill; 1963 Chevy, model by Tim Kolankiewicz.

CONTENTS

INTRODUCTION

The history of American stock car racing is a fascinating journey. From souped-up jalopies on high-speed, midnight runs on dirt roads to packs of brightly decorated, 200 mph corporate billboards on super speedways in just 50 years! It's been quite a ride. And there doesn't seem to be any end in sight. Whether in print, on the radio or live flag-to-flag television broadcasts via satellite, NASCAR racing draws worldwide attention and enjoys unparalleled success.

So too building and detailing scale model race cars reflects an ever-growing desire of model builders to create a personalized piece of American racing history.

Making sense of this ongoing, ever-changing evolution of the American stock-based race car is a simple yet complicated task. This book can only give you a brief snapshot of this phenomenon. Through the building and detailing of scale models you will begin to see the slow and deliberate development of not only the most popular racing series in the world today, but the most active and growing segment of the model car building hobby.

Time Line: The NASCAR Strictly Stock/Grand National/Winston Cup Division

1947—Bill France Sr. chaired the first exploratory meeting to discuss formation of a new major-league sanctioning organization to govern American stock car racing on December 14, 1947, in the lounge of the Streamline Hotel in Daytona Beach, Florida.

1948—The premier event sanctioned by the newly formed National Association for Stock Car Auto Racing (NASCAR) organization was held on February 15, on the combination public highway and beach course along Route 1 and a portion of Daytona Beach at low tide. The race was won by Red Byron in a prewar modified Ford coupe.

1949—A new division called "Strictly Stock," featuring new production-based American cars, held its first race in Charlotte, North Carolina, at the old ¾-mile dirt track. By midyear the Strictly Stock division was renamed Grand National Division. The Oldsmobile division of General Motors triggered a horsepower race by offering their largest-displacement V-8 engine in the smallest and lightest-weight chassis. Headlights and taillights had to be taped over. All passenger doors had to be fastened shut. A popular choice for securing the doors was a leather strap or belt. Red Byron won the very first Grand National (later called Winston Cup) championship in an Oldsmobile 88.

1950—Darlington International Raceway opened for business and hosted their first Grand National event, the Southern 500, the series first-ever super speedway event. That first race was won by Johnny Mantz in a fastback '50 Plymouth coupe. A Ford race car won the company's first GN race in 1950. Bill Rexford captured the championship mostly in an Oldsmobile 88 but clinched the title at Winchester, Indiana, at the wheel of a '49 Ford.

1951—Chrysler Corporation offered the motoring public the first modern, production Hemi-head V-8 engine. Versions were offered in Chryslers and DeSotos first. Hudson Motor company introduced a racing version of their 308 cid in-line flat-head six-cylinder engine called the 7X. Herb Thomas won the 1951 GN championship in a Hudson Hornet.

1952—Hudsons piloted by such legendary drivers as Tim Flock and Herb Thomas dominated the GN circuit this season. While many of the manufacturers had moved on to overhead valve engines, Hudson continued to blow away the competition with its dual-carb flat-head six-cylinder power plant. Tim Flock won the championship in a Hudson Hornet.

1953—As speed and competition increased, roll bars were recommended for all "coupe-style" race cars (those with a door post) and mandatory on all "hardtops" (those without a center door post). Earlier, headlights and taillights had been taped over with masking tape or duct tape; now headlights could be removed, but the resulting hole had to be covered with sheet metal. Dodge won their first GN race in 1953 after receiving their own version of the Hemi-head V-8. Straight exhaust pipes that exited the rear of the race car were recommended by NASCAR. Herb Thomas won his second championship in a Hudson Hornet, marking it three in a row for the independent manufacturer.

1954—Ford and Mercury introduced their first overhead valve V-8 engines. The Ford flat-head V-8 is no longer a competitive power plant in GN racing. An assortment of devices were used to hold hoods and deck lids in a closed position for competition, including bungee cords and threaded nut and bolt hardware. Lee Petty won the championship in a Hemi V-8 powered Chrysler.

1955—Chrysler Corporation introduced the "300," a two-door hardtop powered by a 331 cid Hemi engine with 300 horsepower. Marine magnate (Mercury outboard boat engines) Carl Kiekhaefer fielded a multicar team and dominated the GN series. Plymouth and Pontiac offered their first V-8 engines, but the introduction of the small-block V-8 in the Chevy line changed the face of American motorsports forever. Chevy won its first GN race in 1955. Chevy race teams used the base two-door 150 sedan as the preferred race car body style, though some upscale hardtops and convertibles were also used. Tim Flock won the championship at the wheel of a Kiekhaefer Chrysler 300.

1956—Pete DePaolo of Indy fame was hired by Ford Motor company to organize a factory-supported stock car racing operation. Ford teams ran a variety of body styles including the base two-door sedan, the Crestline two-door hardtop, and on some occasions the top-of-the-line Fairlane two-door hardtop and convertible. Chevy teams primarily chose the 150 and 210 two-door sedan for their race cars. Buck Baker driving a Kiekhaefer Chrysler 300 won the championship.

1957—The classic Ford versus Chevy battle escalated as Ford produced a supercharged 312 V-8 to challenge Chevrolet's small fleet of fuel-injected 283 cid V-8s available in a stripped-down 150 business sedan. Reportedly only ten cars were built by SEDCO (Southern Engineering Development Corporation Operation) in Atlanta, Georgia. They were fondly nicknamed "Black Widows" in part because of their austere black and white paint scheme. Chevy began using truck hubs and six-lug wheels that were part of the race car package until 1963. Before midseason NASCAR banned both supercharging and fuel-injection on GN race cars. Both Ford and Chevys were limited to a single four-barrel carburetor. Ford's two-door sedans of the lowly 300 series as well as Fairlane 500s were used in 1957 competition. Besides the 150 sedans, Chevrolet race cars in 1957 came as 210s and Bel Air two-door hardtops. John Holman and Ralph Moody formed a partnership in Charlotte, North Carolina, next to the municipal airport to assume stock car racing duties for Ford Motor company after Pete DePaolo left the company. Buck Baker drove a 1957 Chevy to the GN championship.

1958—Goodyear joined stalwart Firestone in providing tires for GN racing. Ford and Chevy produced larger engines for increased performance. Ford's was a 352 cid V-8, while the Chevy V-8 engine was available at 348 cid. Lee Petty drove a 1957 Oldsmobile 88 to the championship. The new Chevy body, even with the larger 348 engine, proved not as competitive as the 1957 package. Many ran the '57 Chevy race car for the remainder of the new season. Lee Petty won the second of his three championships in a '57 Oldsmobile.

1959—New Thunderbirds purpose-built by Holman-Moody joined the growing ranks of competitive car brands like Pontiac, Chevrolet, Oldsmobile, Ford, Mercury, Plymouth, and Dodge on the GN circuit. Plymouth offered a new big-block V-8 of 361 cid. The Ford teams relied on the T-birds, as the new '59 Fairlanes were not competitive. The Chevy

teams chose the Impala hardtop, though they did complain of some "lifting" of the rear of the race car at high speed reportedly resulting from the "bat wing" fins. The NASCAR convertible division, started in 1956, disbanded after the 1959 season. Darlington continued to host a special convertible race (Rebel 300) each spring through the 1962 season. Lee Petty captured his third and final NASCAR GN championship driving a new Plymouth, though he had driven a '59 Oldsmobile 88 to victory in the very first Daytona 500 at the newly built Daytona International Speedway in February.

1960—Ford returned to active participation in GN racing and quickly hired the Wood brothers of Stuart, Virginia, to conduct a series of tests of their race cars. Richard Petty won his first race. Robert A. (Junior) Johnson Jr. won the Daytona 500 in a year-old two-door Chevy Biscayne. Tommy Johns was leading the race with a handful of laps left when his year-old Pontiac spun when the rear window popped out. He recovered to finish second. At the very next race the following weekend at Richmond, Virginia, NASCAR mandated rear window straps to keep this from happening again. All production Plymouths and Dodges were now being built on a unibody chassis. Richard Petty finished second in points after coming home third in the Daytona 500. Illinois native Fred Lorenzen came south to work at Holman-Moody and quickly got a ride in a factory Ford race car. Rex White won the GN championship driving a 1960 Chevy Impala hardtop.

1961—The first four-speed transmission appeared in competition as Ford offered it as an option on the new top-of-the-line Galaxie. All engines grew in size in response to the pressure of competition. Fords and Mercurys were now at 390; Plymouth was listed at 413 using the big-block formerly only available in Chryslers and DeSotos; Chevy punched out the 348 to 409 cid and Pontiac covered the field with a whopping 421 cid V-8 engine. Ned Jarrett drove a 348 cid Chevy Bel Air hardtop to the championship.

1962—Ford offered a "Starlift" roof conversion for their factory-backed race cars. The production cars had adopted the Thunderbird-type squared-off roof line, which proved to lack the aerodynamics of the slicker 1961 roof line. NASCAR banned the new roof section after just one event since it was not a production line item. Ford increased the dimensions of its big-block race engine to 406 cid. Ford and Chrysler officially defied the AMA ban on factory support of racing. Joe Weatherly won the championship in a Pontiac Catalina over Richard Petty in a Plymouth. This marked the last time that Pontiacs were a competitive threat in NASCAR for many years.

1963—The Ford Galaxie received a semi-fastback roof line by midyear and another engine displacement boost to 427 cid. Chrysler responded with a 426 cid rendition of their big-block wedge racing engine. After introducing a racing-only V-8 engine called the Mystery 427 Mark VI, Chevrolet hastily withdrew factory support, concerned about their violation of the AMA racing ban, leaving the Chevrolet teams to fend for themselves. Bungee cords and wing nuts securing hoods and deck lids became a thing of the past as NASCAR mandated a positive locking device and hood pins became the hardware of choice. Hood pins were in common use by some teams as early as 1960. Eight-inch-high numerals indicating horsepower ratings were required on both sides of the hood. A single bucket seat of factory origin was also required, as was a single horizontal brace on both sides of the roll cage. Fords and Mercurys continued to route their exhaust dumps through the side frame rails, thereby allowing a cleaner air flow under the race cars. Joe Weatherly, without a regular ride most of the season, drove for eight different teams and repeated as champion in a Mercury.

1964—The '64 season is one of great triumph and devastating tragedy. Chrysler introduced the 426 Hemi engine and blew the competition away on the super speedways. Richard Petty won his first of seven Daytona 500s. Ford countered with a high-rise 427 engine and threatened to produce an even more awesome race engine with Hemi-heads and overhead camshafts. To regulate the power struggle, NASCAR mandated that cars with 114-inch wheelbases were limited to 396 cid. Cars of 116-inch wheelbase were limited to 428 inches of displacement. Reigning champ Joe Weatherly was killed in the season opener at Riverside. Second place Daytona 500 finisher Jimmy Pardue was killed testing the new inner liner tire for Goodyear at Charlotte in September. Likewise, 1963 Rookie-of-the-year Billy Wade was killed testing tires at Daytona, and Glen "Fireball" Roberts was gravely burned during a crash at the World 600 at Charlotte and died of complications a month later. Three horizontal bars were now required on the driver's side of roll cage along with the one earlier mandated for the right side. NASCAR banned the practice of routing the exhaust dump pipes through the side frame rails, citing safety concerns. Richard Petty beat out Ned Jarrett to win his first of seven championships.

1965—Tire inner liners and fuel cells with foam "bladders" were adopted during the 1965 season. All engines were limited to 427 inches displacement. All nonproduction engines were banned from competition including the Chrysler Hemi, Ford single overhead cam, and all "stagger"-valve engines. Ford applauded the move, while Chrysler withdrew from competition until rules were modified in late season. Treaded race tires grew in width again to 9 inches. Minimum weight was mandated at 3900 pounds. Ned Jarrett won his second and last championship, this time in a '65 Ford Galaxie.

1966—NASCAR consented to the use of Hemi and single overhead cam (SOHC) engines in the series but limited them to the largest cars in each manufacturer's line. All Ford and Chrysler engines used a single four-barrel carburetor while (GM) stagger-valve wedge engines could use two carbs. This was done in hopes that GM would abandon their corporate ban on racing. It didn't work. After Chrysler's boycott in '65, Ford, unhappy with the new rules, withdrew from competition after the eighth race of the season in March at Atlanta. The Ford SOHC V-8 never saw action in a competitive NASCAR event. Four horizontal driver-side roll cage bars were required for 1966. Dual brake master cylinders were now required on all cars. Shoulder harnesses and approved crash helmets, recommended in the past, were mandated for 1966. The very first deck spoiler was permitted on the new Dodge Charger. It was only one inch in height. This season marked the first use of body templates. Factory-backed Ford and Mercury race cars returned late in the season in the form of big-block powered Fairlanes and Comets. These cars were the forerunners of the modern NASCAR Busch Grand National and Winston Cup race car, featuring the merging of a reinforced unibody platform with the front frame clip from the 1965–66 Holman-Moody Galaxie. They were commonly referred to as "half-chassis" race cars. Minimum weight was now determined by the rule of 9.36 pounds per cubic inch of engine displacement. David Pearson, driving a Cotton Owens prepared Dodge Charger, won his first of three championships.

1967—Two horizontal side bars were now mandated for the passenger side of the roll cage. Front disk-type brakes were permitted for the first time. Chrysler Hemi engines were limited to one four-barrel carb, and their wedge engines could use two four-barrels or three two-barrels. Ford was allowed to use two four-barrel carbs on their tunnel-port 427 cid race engine. Minimum weight was now 3500 pounds. Production chrome trim was required around the front windshield, and production intake manifolds were required on all race engines. Stock production-based frames were no longer required. Teams could build race cars with fully fabricated frames that resembled a stock frame for safety reasons. Eighteen-inch-high numerals were required on the rear deck. David Pearson left the Cotton Owen's Dodge to replace the retired Fred Lorenzen in a Holman-Moody Ford. Richard Petty recorded his second championship while setting an all-time win record of 27 season victories and ten of those in a row.

1968—Chrysler Hemi-engine cars were permitted two four-barrel carbs after Ford's new aerodynamic twins, the Torino and Mercury Cyclone, swept the top positions in the Daytona 500. As Ford had learned, the advantage that could not be achieved through sheer horsepower could be gained with increased aerodynamics. The smaller and slicker Ford and Mercury bodies were extremely fast, even with the old but potent 427 tunnel port engine. David Pearson, after switching in mid-1967 from a Dodge Charger to a Holman-Moody Ford, won his second of three championships.

1969—To combat the very fast and successful corporate twins from Ford, Dodge introduced a tweaked version of the '69 Charger called the "500," featuring a flush grille (actually the grille from a '68 Coronet mounted flush with the front of the grille opening) and a flush-mounted rear window replacing the deeply recessed unit on the standard Charger. Ford countered this move with their own "slippery ship," the Talledega, featuring a drooped nose. It also included a flush-mounted grille and a front bumper that was actually a slightly reshaped Torino rear bumper. A few weeks later, Mercury had their own version of the car called Cyclone Spoiler II, which was released at the same time as a new Boss 429 Ford Hemi race engine. The new race motor carried a whopping 1040 cfm Dominator carb. Wheel width increased to 9 inches with a 10-inch tire width. Four horizontal side bars were now required for the passenger side of the roll cage. Dry sump oil systems were permitted for the first time, allowing the engine to be mounted lower in the chassis and reducing oil spillage on the track from blown engines. A few teams tried two-way radios at Talledega, and slick tires (no tread) were used for the first time in competition at the same facility. David Pearson won his third and final championship at the wheel of a Holman-Moody Ford Torino.

1970—NASCAR moved to tighten control on specialty race cars like those from Ford, Mercury, and Dodge. New rules mandated that at least 1000 examples be built for street use. Plymouth complied with the letter of the law, introducing the Superbird and luring Richard Petty away from Ford. Ford Motor Company reduced its racing budget by 75 percent. While Dodge and Plymouth continued using the venerable 426 Hemi, Ford now had three racing engines, the 427 tunnel port/side oiler, the 428, and the 429 Hemi. Ford continued to race its '69 specialty cars, as did Dodge, because of better aerodynamics, though the '70 models were seen occasionally on short tracks and road courses. Fuel fillers were located on the left side of race cars for ovals and the right side for road courses. All exhaust dumps were mandated to exit in front of the rear wheels. Wheel width increased to 9.5 inches and tire width increased to 12.1 inches. Firestone withdrew from NASCAR racing. After Richard Petty's horrific crash at Darlington during the Southern 500, window nets were mandated for all events for next season, and side glass was outlawed. The first window nets were made of a type of netting material. Windshield retainer clips were now mandated, two at the bottom and three at the top. Door handles now had to be removed and the openings covered with a metal plate. Headlight openings could now be used as air intakes for brake cooling. Head rests with padding were now mandated. Rear deck lid numbers were still required, as well as smaller numbers on the right front and right rear tail- and headlight covers. Bobby Isaac won the championship in a K and K Insurance-sponsored Dodge Charger.

1971—All specialty cars were limited to 5-liter (305 cid) engines. Dick Brooks wheeled a small-block Charger Daytona in the Daytona 500. This marked the last competitive appearance for these types of cars. Six-liter (366 cid) small-block engines were now allowed along with the big-block race engines. The large-displacement engines were required to use carb restrictor plates at all events. All makes of cars were restricted to using engines available as factory equipment. Chrysler Corporation drastically reduced factory support and only backed the Petty operation, which fielded Plymouths for Richard Petty and Dodge Chargers for Buddy Baker. Junior Johnson, no longer getting factory support from Ford, convinced Chevrolet to return to NASCAR. Johnson built the first Monte Carlo and hired Charlie Glotzbach to drive. Richard Howard of Charlotte Motor Speedway financed the operation. Fire extinguishers were mandated for all race cars and flameproof driving suits for all drivers. Goodyear began stenciling the word "Goodyear" on the side walls of their racing tires. Prior to this the side-wall lettering on street and racing tires was the same. Richard Petty in a Plymouth won his third NASCAR championship title.

1972—R. J. Reynolds Company agreed to become the series sponsor. All races of 250 miles or longer were scheduled as Winston Cup Series. The schedule was reduced from 50-plus events to just 31. American Motors Corporation entered NASCAR racing. Roger Penske campaigned Holman-Moody–built Matadors with Mark Donahue at the wheel. After Chrysler Corporation withdrew from the series, Richard Petty signed a long-term contract with STP Corporation. Petty Enterprises fielded Plymouths and Dodges for Richard and Dodge Chargers for Buddy Baker. Bud Moore, fresh from fielding Mustangs in SCCA Trans-Am series, built a '72 Torino powered by a Ford 351 cid Cleveland small-block engine for the car. The '72 Fords and Mercurys reverted to body-on-frame construction featuring coil springs with trailing arm suspension at the rear. With Ford withdrawing from NASCAR racing, John Holman and Ralph Moody called it quits and parted company. Richard Petty, driving both Plymouths and Dodge Chargers, won his fourth championship.

1973—Mark Donahue drove the AMC/Penske Matador to its first victory by winning the season opener at Riverside. The car was equipped with four-wheel disk brakes and the other competitors converted quickly. The large-displacement engines were further restricted to using the smallest carb available. This was the last season for these behemoths. The sealed ram-air system, in which the rear of the air cleaner is attached to an opening in the firewall at the base of the cowl vents, was outlawed. Free-standing air cleaners became the standard. Displaying the engine displacement numbers on the hood of race cars was optional. Requiring the car number to be displayed on the rear deck lid was dropped. Benny Parsons, driving a Chevrolet Chevelle and a Monte Carlo, won his first and only championship title.

1974—Aircraft-style dry break fuel fillers were permitted. The use of electronic ignition systems was allowed. The openings between the body sheet metal and bumpers had to be covered with sheet metal. The first "NASCAR-generic" chassis rules were adopted. No longer would a race car have to be built with the type of suspension pieces used on the production model. All makes of race cars could use coil springs, leaf springs, or torsion bars as suspension components. Driving a Dodge Charger, Richard Petty won his fifth NASCAR championship title.

1975—Chevrolet introduced the slope-nose Laguna S-3 version of the Chevelle two-door coupe. Engine size was recalibrated to 358 cid, the dimensions still used today. Rules permitted the removal of crash impact equipment from between the body and bumpers, allowing them to be mounted closer for better aerodynamics. AMC withdrew from NASCAR after the '75 season. Driving his trusty STP Dodge Charger, Richard Petty won his sixth NASCAR championship.

1976—Dodge won its last race in NASCAR in '76. Penske switched to Mercury sheet metal and power for the '76 season. But this was not the final chapter for the Matador. Cale Yarborough, driving a Junior Johnson–prepped Chevrolet, won the first of his three championship titles.

1977—NASCAR expanded the eligibility rules from three years to four for 1977. Richard Petty continued to campaign his 1974 Dodge Charger. This was the last year of eligibility for the Chevrolet Laguna S-3. It would join the Talledega, Spoiler II, Superbird, and Daytona in the history books. Bobby Allison returned to the series with his own operation, campaigning AMC Matadors once more and with sponsorship from First National City Travelers Checks. Cale Yarborough repeated as champion, driving Chevrolet Lagunas and Monte Carlos to victory.

1978—Centrifugal forces as the result of increasing corner velocities at high-speed tracks like Talledega caused Goodyear to resort to slick tires for predicable adhesion. Even the most minute amount of tread on the race tire contact patch caused a 3800-pound race car at 200 mph to get

very twitchy. For all but the dedicated Ford teams, the race cars of choice for almost everyone else was the '77 Oldsmobile Cutlass-S and the trusty '77 Chevrolet Monte Carlo. The Olds featured an angular nose very reminiscent of the recently departed Laguna. No '78 GM body styles were used in NASCAR's premiere division because of the corporate-wide downsizing restricting their most popular two-door coupes to 108-inch wheelbases against a NASCAR-mandated 115 inches in the rule book. NASCAR adopted a "corporate" engine policy, thereby allowing Buick, Oldsmobile, and Pontiac bodied race cars to compete. The corporate engine was more specifically the Chevrolet 350 cid-based small-block V-8. Cale Yarborough captured his third and final NASCAR championship, driving an Oldsmobile Cutlass and a Monte Carlo.

1979—Adjustable shock absorbers and rubber coil spring inserts were now permitted. Richard Petty piloted a '77 Monte Carlo, '79 Caprice, and '77 Cutlass to win his seventh and final NASCAR championship. It was the closet finish yet to that point, with Petty taking the title by just 11 points over Darrell Waltrip.

1980—The official NASCAR frame (360 degree roll cage/chassis structure) became the standard way race cars were constructed for the series. The whole structure was fabricated from scratch, and the sheet metal pieces were then fastened in place on the chassis/roll cage structure. Earlier, a sheet metal shell was constructed and the reinforcing was then assembled inside this structure. Doors no longer had to be removable. Dale Earnhardt, driving a 1977 Monte Carlo, captured his first of seven NASCAR championships.

1981—NASCAR finally recognized the new smaller, downsized production cars and adjusted the rules governing the dimensions of WC race cars accordingly. The mandated wheelbase of 115 inches was reduced to 110 inches, even though all eligible makes were being produced on 108-inch wheelbases. Production hood and rear deck hinges were no longer required. Exposed hinges were mandated. Big-block engines were deleted from the rule book. Contingency sponsor decal placement is specifically regulated by the sanctioning body. Three steel straps were mandated to hold the front windshield in place. The word "Eagle" first appeared on the sidewall of Goodyear racing tires. Darrell Waltrip drove a Junior Johnson–owned Buick Regal to the first of his three championships.

1982—Darrell Waltrip repeated as champion again driving the familiar Mountain Dew Buick Regal. The premiere NASCAR circuit adopted the name "Winston Cup Series." The former series name "Grand National" was applied to the newly reorganized Sportsman series.

1983—Ford Motor Company introduced the new aero Thunderbird with greatly improved aerodynamics over the virtually bricklike '81–'82 model. Chevrolet, not to be upstaged, responded with a special droop-nose version of its Monte Carlo called the SS. All electrical switches were required to be on the dashboard panel. NASCAR mandated the reduction of the header dump pipe diameter from 4 to 3½ inches. Requiring the display of cubic inch markings on the hood was deleted from the rule book. Bobby Allison drove a Buick Regal for DiGard Racing team to win his only WC championship title.

1984—Richard Petty won his 200th race by beating Cale Yarborough to the flag at the Firecracker 400 in Daytona. Terry Labonte won his first of two NASCAR titles to date (the second title coming in 1996) at the wheel of the Piedmont Airlines Monte Carlo.

1985—Dual master brake cylinders were required on all race cars. Darrell Waltrip drove a Budweiser Monte Carlo to his third and final championship title.

1986—Plexiglas rear windows were now permitted and had to be mounted flush with the window opening. The recommended location for the battery, which over the years had moved from under the hood to the trunk area, was now in a housing behind the driver's seat. All driveshafts had to be painted white for clearer visibility in case they became separated from the race car. No pump motors or electrical motors were permitted in the trunk area. GM responded to the success of the new Thunderbird with an aero package of their own. The Chevrolet MC received a fastback-style rear window glass. The Pontiac Grand Prix received a new droop nose plus a similar fastback window glass to the MC. The new Pontiac is called the "2 + 2." Driving a "bubble-back" Monte Carlo, Dale Earnhardt won the second of his seven championship titles.

1987—Ford introduced a revised T-bird body shell featuring a more pointed beaklike front end and a revised roof line. This resulted in a slightly higher rear deck height, which raised the rear spoiler up further into the airflow over the race car at high speed. Bobby Allison survived a frightening crash at Talladega in his Buick LeSabre. As a result of this crash—not only to slow the race cars down but to keep them from literally taking flight—NASCAR mandated two parallel roof rails, a passenger-side window and passenger-side body skirt stretching between the front and rear wheel openings. These changes were required at Daytona and Talladega events starting in the 1988 season. Many teams converted their race car chassis to use single Bilstein shock absorbers on all four corners. Dale Earnhardt won his third title driving a Monte Carlo.

1988—Chrome wheels were no longer permitted in competition. Many teams began using Bassett nine-hole wheels with their distinctive black finish and thin red line around the rim. Pontiac introduced a newly restyled Grand Prix body shell. The short rear deck surface didn't allow for sufficient down force, and the cars were initially very squirrely. Hoosier, a small Indiana-based racing tire manufacturer, joined ranks with Goodyear to provide tires for the Winston Cup circuit. Midway through the season some teams began using two valve stems on each tire rim. The second valve stem was used to inflate the safety inner liner. Bill Elliott drove the Coors Thunderbird to his first championship to date.

1989—Chevrolet introduced the MC replacement, the Lumina, at the Winston 500 at Talladega, even though the two-door version of the car was not available to the public until fall. The final appearance of the Monte Carlo was the 500-mile event at Martinsville, Virginia. Roof rails were now required at all NASCAR racetracks. In a surprise announcement, Hoosier tires withdrew midway through the season. Rusty Wallace drove a Raymond Beadle–owned Pontiac to his first NASCAR championship.

1990—Dale Earnhardt won his fourth title driving the Goodwrench Lumina.

1991—A change in the lateral support bar in the roll cage was mandated for 1991. Driver's seats were now mandated to have padded rib protectors and leg extensions on both sides. Buick Motor Division of General Motors withdrew from competition at the close of the '91 season.

1992—NASCAR mandated that no onboard computer or telemetry equipment would be permitted during competition. Disk brakes were now mandated as a requirement on all race cars. A minimum 45 degree angle was mandated as the standard on all rear deck spoilers. At the final event of the season at Atlanta, Goodyear introduced new sidewall lettering printed in yellow and reading "Goodyear, Eagle, #1," replacing the earlier lettering printed in white. The change from white to yellow lettering denoted the change from bias-ply to radial racing tire construction. Oldsmobile division of General Motors withdrew from competition at the conclusion of the '92 season. Two parallel rails running down the rear window and across the rear deck lid were mandated in a further attempt to keep the cars from taking flight. Alan Kulwicki beat out Bill Elliott by just 10 points to capture his only WC title, the closest finish in history.

1993—Tragedy struck the sport as defending champ Kulwicki was killed in a plane crash near Bristol, Tennessee, the first day of April. Later that year, Davey Allison was also killed in a helicopter accident at Talledega. Passenger-side windows and side skirts were now required on all NASCAR tracks 1.5 miles or longer. Race cars must run without side glass on all short tracks. Dale Earnhardt won his sixth championship driving the GM Goodwrench Lumina.

1994—Roof flaps and cowl flaps were instituted as the newest device in attempting to keep the race cars upright and on the ground. Roof and cowl flaps were mandatory on all tracks of one mile or longer. Hoosier tires returned to the series and provided tires for selected teams. Dale Earnhardt won his seventh championship in the number three Lumina.

1995—Chevrolet reintroduced the Monte Carlo name plate and the race car proved to be a nearly unbeatable success. Hoosier tires did not return to the series in '95. NASCAR allowed the Pontiac Grand Prix teams to stretch the body shell by some five inches and permitted the reconfiguring of the silhouette to more closely resemble that of the T-bird and brand-new Monte Carlo. Roof flaps were now mandatory at all NASCAR racetracks. Roof flaps (and cowl flaps) proved so effective that the rear deck and right-side rear window rails were eliminated. Currently, all race cars carry a single rail strip only on the driver's side of the rear window. Jeff Gordon, driving a new Monte Carlo, captured his first WC championship title.

1996—Pontiac introduced a new Grand Prix based on the Chevrolet Monte Carlo body shell. Terry Labonte captured his second championship in a Monte Carlo, making him the driver with the longest period (12 years) between titles.

1997—Rules change called for the addition of a vertical roll cage bar, dead center of the windshield, perpendicular to the dashboard. Heat extraction vents in the quarter windows were disallowed. Fresh air NACA-style inlets were still okay to use. The chin spoiler's horizontal width (from side to side) was now restricted to the outside width of the front tire treads. A new style of air cleaner housing attaching to the firewall only accepted incoming air flow through the cowl vent.

IN THE BEGINNING

BUILDING AND DETAILING A NASCAR MODIFIED '40 FORD COUPE

This 1940 Ford built by John Wise is very typical of the production-based race cars so popular after World War II.

American stock cars came in various shapes and took many directions during the 1930s and '40s. After World War II, the public was hungry for anything automotive and motor racing shot toward the top of the list. In 1947 Bill France, a northern entrepreneur and racer, established the foundation of an event that has become number one in spectator attendance of any motorsports series on this planet.

Many credit the souped-up coupes and sedans employed so effectively in the southeast during this period as transportation for the preferred corn cash crop—"white lightning"—as the basic platform of this sport. In such chronicles as Alex Gabbard's *Return to Thunder Road*, tales of the exploits and

derring-do of determined men and rapid machinery are legendary.

As the story goes, enterprising promoters lured these "competitors" out of the "holler" and onto circular paths in a neighborhood pasture. The object was to settle once and for all the verbal feuding as to who was the "baddest" car and driver in these here parts!

After Bill France and his associates met in Daytona Beach, Florida, laying the groundwork for a centralized sanctioning body with fair, equitable, and consistent rules, the new organization, the National Association for Stock Car Auto Racing (NASCAR), set about to present their first event. This turned out to be a race for modified stock cars on the old Daytona

Beach highway-beach course. The very popular '36, '37, '38, '39 and '40 Ford coupes dominated this early event. They were plentiful, cheap, and powered by a stout little flat-head V-8 engine. Additionally, there existed a boatload of aftermarket speed equipment for these engines.

Join us now as John Wise shows how to construct a replica of one of the earliest NASCAR race cars. For this project you need an Ertl/AMT '40 Ford coupe, Testor's Model Master gloss black paint, wheels and tires from the Ertl/AMT '36 Ford, and Plastruct and Evergreen plastic materials. For this building project, I drew the decals on my Macintosh home computer using a Pagemaker layout

Fig. 1-1. By combining parts from the Ertl/AMT 1939 Tudor sedan or a '40 coupe you can build this model as a '39 or a '40. Use the '39 hood, grille, and fenders from the sedan kit with the coupe body to make the '39 coupe. John Wise built this model from the box as a '40 business coupe.

Fig. 1-3. Repeat the process for the driver's door on the left side of the body shell. Here John found the task a bit more challenging, pointing out that the plastic is rather thin along the radius of the door frame above the vent window. If you see any unsightly and uneven gaps around the new opening with the door in place, a short section of .010 sheet plastic glued into place and sanded to shape will take care of them.

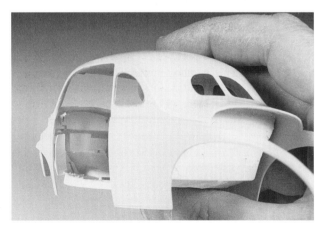

Fig. 1-4. Install the interior inside the body shell. You'll also have to cut out the interior door panel to match the door opening. Once that's done, your next step is to construct door jambs and sills. Seen here is the front door jamb.

Fig. 1-2. To open and hinge the rear deck lid, start by scribing along the seam lines separating the deck lid from the surrounding body panels. Use the back side of a fresh no. 11 X-Acto blade. Work slowly, stay in the groove, and make many low-pressure passes. If you have taken your time in scribing open the trunk lid, it should look like this. Of course, the less material you remove while scribing, the less shimming you'll need to get the trunk lid to fit the new opening properly. Also, carefully shave away a small amount of material along the leading edge of the rear body panel along the new opening. This will allow the lid to open more freely.

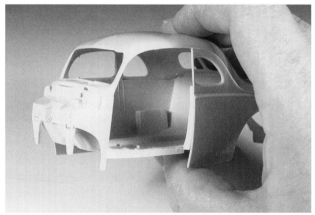

Fig. 1-5. Make a rear door jamb and lower door sill as shown here and glue it to the new door opening in the side of the interior. With everything in place, there should be no unsightly gaps between body and interior. You may want to make a hinge for the driver's door using two pieces of brass rod bent into an L and inserted into a length of plastic tubing. Mount the tubing behind the front door jamb panel. Then drill two corresponding .020″ holes in the leading edge of the door. Next, insert the brass wire L brackets into the tubing (do not glue) and glue them to the holes in the door. You can use this same type of hinge on the rear deck lid.

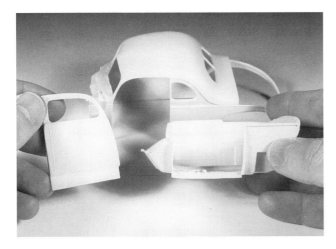

Figs. 1-6 and 1-7. Next, glue the interior door panel into place on the inside surface of the driver's door. You might wish to use regular plastic glue that takes a while to dry. This will permit you time to align the panel properly before the cement sets. Use

body filler on both the front and rear edges to fill in the seam between the exterior and interior door panels. A final test-fit is now in order. Use a bit of body filler to clean up the seam along the floorboard.

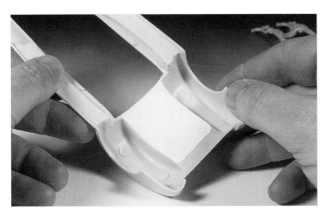

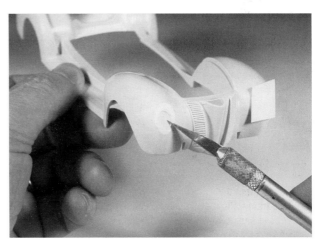

Fig. 1-8. With the trunk area now exposed with the opening of the lid, fill in the depressions in the rear surface of the interior bucket to give it a more finished appearance. Use .010 sheet plastic to form an interior trunk floor. The plastic is thin enough that it can bend to the contour of the rear inner fender structure. This will also provide a horizontal surface for mounting the racing fuel tank.

Fig. 1-9. Rules for this type of modified race car allowed for the complete removal of the head- and taillights. Fill in the openings with micro-balloons and super glue. Dr. Micro Tool body filler is also a good choice for filling in the taillight openings. File and sand the area smooth. You need a flat surface where the stock headlight would normally be mounted. The quickest way to fill in the fender opening is to simply super glue a piece of .020 sheet plastic over the opening. Trim the sheet stock to the approximate shape with an X-Acto knife, then file and sand to the contour of the fender.

Fig. 1-10. Here is a view of before (bottom) and after (top) the chassis modifications. Trim away the floorboard between the frame rails where the stock exhaust is molded in. Use the openings in the floorboard as a template to cut out pieces of .020 sheet stock to replace the floorboard. Some filing and sanding may be needed to achieve a precise fit. Glue the new panels into place.

Fig. 1-11. John recommends brushing flat black bottle paint onto areas where you've made modifications. Careful sanding reveals if they need further finishing. In the case of the engine and transmission, the flat black paint works as a final filler of the large seam down the middle of the two halves. The major parts of this modified are ready for priming and painting.

program. Once the artwork was completed I generated a laser printer copy. Then a local sign shop silk-screened water-slide decals onto Detail Master blank decal sheets. Though at this time there are no specific water-slide decals for this model, you can come reasonably close using Woodland Scenics dry-transfer lettering.

John Wise finished the model with Model Master gloss black. The interior and chassis are painted Testor's flat black. The engine components are finished in shades of steel, aluminum, and gunmetal. The radiator is painted copper. The wheel are painted gloss white and gloss black.

Reference material for this near-replica NASCAR modified stock car can be found in the December 1988 issue of *Circle Track* magazine. This model is fashioned after the National Modified Championship race car owned and driven by the late Gober Sosebee. With a single carb running on pump gas he competed in the Sportsman series. By changing the intake manifold to accept three carbs and filling the tank with alcohol, Sosebee ran the coupe as a modified.

2

FAST FIFTY-SEVENS

BUILDING AND DETAILING STOCK CARS FROM THE MID-'50S

Build Tom Dill's 1957 Ford supercharged 300 NASCAR stocker by combining an All-American Models resin kit with parts from an Ertl/AMT '57 Fairlane 500. Paint is authentic mid-'50s Ford colors, and the markings are from Fred Cady Design.

By 1957 Ford and in turn Chevrolet realized that success on the racetrack was responsible for generating showroom traffic. As the old adage goes, "what wins on Sunday, sells on Monday!" Many body styles of both makes competed during this period. The Ford brigade is probably best remembered for the short-lived supercharged 312 cid V-8 engines, which were predominately used in the baseline 300 series two-door post sedan.

Likewise, Chevrolet had their own not-so-secret weapon in the form of a baseline 150 post sedan powered by the new Corvette fuel-injected V-8 and commonly referred to as the "Black

Widow." Reference materials on these two celebrated cars may be found as follows:

1957 Ford 300
Circle Track magazine

1957 Chevrolet "Black Widow"
Super Chevy magazine
November, 1995

1957 Chevrolet "Black Widow"
Hot Rod magazine
August, 1987

1957 Chevrolet "Black Widow"
Motor Racing Replica News
Issue 10, 1992

NASCAR reacted quickly and decisively by outlawing both limited-production models from Ford and Chevrolet. Ford (and sister division Mercury) and arch-rival Chevrolet were both forced by the rules to utilize single four-barrel carburetors on their racing engines for the bulk of the 1957 season. Fuel injection and supercharging have not been allowed on NASCAR race cars since.

In the mid-'50s Ford used a variety of body styles in stock car racing. Frequently seen in racing trim for Ford was the two-door sedan and hardtop coupe as well as the convertible. Both the stripped-down base models and top-of-the-line luxury models were used by Ford and Mercury teams as race cars. The same was true for Chevrolet—everything from the 150 businessman's two-door coupe to the 210 Bel Air hardtop and convertible were adapted for stock car racing. The following production plastic injection-molded kits can be used to build an accurate mid-'50s NASCAR stocker:

• Ertl/AMT '57 Chevrolet two-door hardtop
• Revell '57 Chevrolet Bel Air hardtop
• Ertl/AMT '57 Ford hardtop

Currently there are a few water-slide decal sheets available making it possible to build race car models from these kits:

• Wood brothers' '57 Fords
• Buck Bakers' '57 Chevrolet convertible
• Fireball Roberts's '57 supercharged Ford
• Jack Smith's '57 Chevrolet "Black Widow"
• Paul Goldsmith's '57 Chevrolet and '57 Ford

All of these decal sheets are from Fred Cady Design.

Three of the models shown here were built from aftermarket resin pieces requiring parts from one of the plastic kits listed above. Tom Dill's '57 Ford 300 two-door sedan is a product of All-American Models. His '57 Mercury convertible is modified from a hardtop manufactured by The Modelhaus. Carl Rees built this '57 Chevy "Black Widow" using a resin conversion kit from All-American models.

Resin works very much like polystyrene, being pliable and responding to fillers and all types of glue and bonding agents intended for regular kit plastics. Resin can be filed, sanded, and cut using the very same tools used for styrene plastics. One distinct advantage resin has is its compatibility with automotive surfacers, fillers, and primers and acrylic enamels and lacquers. Polystyrene plastic always requires a primer-barrier coat, as automotive finishes attack the unprotected surfaces of the plastic. Resin does not.

Let's take a brief look at three vintage race car models that will be built using resin cast parts.

1957 Ford supercharged 300

Things you will need to augment the All-American conversion kit include items from the Ertl/AMT '57 Fairlane 500 plastic kit, automotive paint from Model Car World, and of course decals from Cady Design.

But first, resin parts do differ from injection-molded plastic in that they carry a mold release that must be removed. You can soak parts in Wesley's tire cleaner or scrub them thoroughly with a strong household cleaner like Soft Scrub. Neglecting to clean resin parts thoroughly will virtually guarantee that neither paint nor glue will stick to the surface. A good test is to stick a piece of masking tape onto the part. If it takes some effort to peel the tape off the part, you have cleaned it sufficiently.

The interior, dash, steering wheel, and front seat come from the Ertl/AMT kit. First remove the horn ring from the steering wheel. Next remove the passenger-side back of the bench-style seat. Fill in the opening in the rear of the seat cushion with .020 sheet plastic. Build a simple four-point roll bar from 5/32″ plastic rod. The red and white interior color scheme is carried over from the two-tone exterior. When the pieces are painted and thoroughly dry to the touch, install the roll bar to the interior floor between the front and back seats.

You may have to remove a bit of flash, left by the casting process, from the resin chassis. Also, fill any small air bubbles with micro-balloons and super glue or fill them carefully with thickened primer applied with a small-diameter brush. Repeat this process until any holes are filled or scabbed over with primer. Then sand the primed surfaces smooth. Next attach front and rear suspension components from the Ertl/AMT kit into their proper locations according to the kit instructions. Assemble the V-8 engine from the

Ertl/AMT kit according to kit instructions and paint it as shown. It is always an excellent idea to periodically test-fit component parts before final assembly. Checking to see if the plastic engine/transmission fits into the resin chassis is a good starting point.

Spray-paint the chassis flat black and do the exhaust system in contrasting metallic paint colors. Brush-paint the suspension parts with either gloss or matte black paint to contrast with the flat finish of the chassis.

Use the plastic kit hood and engine compartment components like the battery, radiator, and firewall from the Ertl/AMT kit. Prime and paint the kit hood along with the resin body two-tone red and white. Use Bare-Metal chrome foil to do the bright work on the body shell.

Cady decals require the builder to register each layer by hand. Many times this not a bad idea—you will appreciate this feature the next time you use a set of preregistered decals that is not properly registered. Apply the first layer of decals in various locations and allow them to dry completely. Applying a second layer too soon will result in the first layer loosening and then you'll be wrestling with multiple layers at the same time.

1957 Mercury convertible

The Modelhaus 1957 Mercury is very unusual in that no previous model existed of this significant automobile until the resin kit came along. Tom Dill modified the stock hardtop into a convertible race car. Building a curbside version would have been a task, but Tom wasn't satisfied to stop there.

After cutting the top off the Mercury Monterey with a razor saw, you'll have to make a tonneau cover for the interior. Cover the extreme rear of the interior with a piece of .020 sheet plastic the shape of the stock package shelf. The pliable section of the tonneau was made from a thin scrap piece of naugahyde. (You can find it at an auto trim shop.) Use the interior opening in the body as a basic template to form

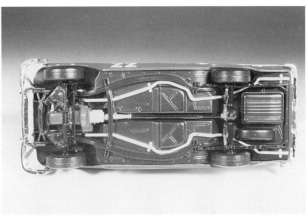

The Ford 300 engine compartment. Note the Paxton supercharged 312 cid V-8 power plant and the rather stock-appearing engine compartment accessories. Paint the '57 300 chassis flat black. You can also make effective use of semigloss and gloss black finishes on suspension components and shades of metallic paint on the exhaust system.

these two pieces. Next, fashion a roll bar from 5/32″ plastic rod.

The resin Merc comes with a full interior, including seats, dashboard, and steering wheel. Cut the horn ring from the stock wheel and also remove the passenger-side seat back from the resin front seat.

The Modelhaus resin chassis has all the vital suspension and drive line parts depicted in relief. You could build this model as a curbside and simply highlight the chassis by detail-painting the individual components. Tom opened up the engine bay and cut away the front portion of the frame, removing the entire front suspension. He replaced this with the steerable front suspension and corresponding frame pieces from an Ertl/AMT 1957 Ford kit.

Likewise, grind away the entire molded-in rear axle and leaf springs at the rear of the resin chassis. Transplant separate individual parts like the rear axle and springs from the '57 Ford kit into place on the Merc chassis. The engine and transmission along with core support, radiator, and battery come from the plastic kit.

Scratchbuild the firewall from sheet plastic. Make the unique Mercury valve covers from plastic bar stock cut in lengths to fit the Ford

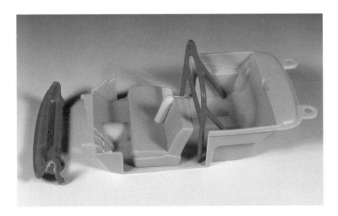

Take the interior bucket, dash, and steering wheel for the '57 Ford 300 from the Ertl/AMT '57 Fairlane 500. Leave out the rear seat, remove the passenger's-side seat back, and add a driver's seat bolster. Remember to fill in the back of the passenger's seat cushion with sheet plastic and add a driver's-side bolster. Make a simple four-point roll bar from 5/32″ plastic rod. Measure the distance from the interior floor to the inside of the top of the body with the interior installed. Some height adjustment may be necessary to get just the right fit for the roll bar.

The body gets a two-tone paint job. Keep the edges of your masking material burnished down and sharp to ensure a clean parting line. If any paint creeps under the masking material, you can usually scrape it away carefully with a sharp X-Acto blade. Apply the decals one layer at a time, making sure they are lined up straight. Allow plenty of drying time before moving on to the next decal layer. Since the hood opens and closes, attach it to the body and see how it travels. Be certain that there's enough clearance, so you don't scrape or chip paint off the edges after final assembly.

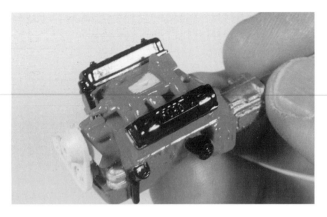

Accurate detail-painting of the engine and transmission adds to the realistic look. Here the engine block is painted Testor's Ford Engine Red. The use of gloss black, aluminum, and steel paint colors on engine accessories is appropriate.

Tom Dill's 1957 Tim Flock Mercury convertible built from a Modelhaus resin kit. The model features an opening hood, detailed V-8 engine, steerable front suspension, and computer-generated dry-transfer markings. The basic engine came from an Ertl/AMT '57 Ford plastic kit, and the dual four-barrel carbs and intake manifold came from the same company's '56 Ford Victoria kit. The finished chassis on this '57 Mercury convertible features a steerable front suspension and a rear suspension transplanted from the Ertl/AMT '57 Ford Fairlane plastic kit.

cylinder heads. Then hand-score the fins and carefully hand-cut the stylized M on each valve cover from .010 plastic sheet.

Score the hood lines with an X-Acto blade to open this panel on the resin body. Use brass wire and small-diameter plastic tubing to make a pair of hinges allowing the hood to open and close. Note that the hood is hinged to the front, as it was on the full-size car.

Tires for this famous Daytona beach course winner are also resin from the Modelhaus. The wheels are homemade. Dill cast resin copies of the open

wheels from the original AMT 1957 Ford plastic kit.

Create the red, white, and blue paint scheme with Mercury automotive lacquers of the mid-'50s. The individual colors are available from MCW finishes. You can do some of the small lettering by hand, but the bulk of the markings for this Merc were generated on a computer and output as dry transfers. A local sign shop was able to scan photos of the race car into a computer drawing program. From those electronic images, graphics were sized and shaped to fit the 1/25 scale model.

1957 Chevrolet "Black Widow"

Carl Rees built this replica starting with a resin conversion kit from All-American Models. The kit includes a modified 150 series body shell, chassis (with exhaust system removed), modified interior bucket, dashboard, four six-lug wheels and vacuum-formed window glass.

An Ertl/AMT 1957 Chevrolet Bel Air hardtop kit is necessary as a parts donor. From this kit you'll need the front grille/bumper, rear bumper, head- and taillights, front and rear suspension, differential and drive shaft, hood and rear deck ornaments, front

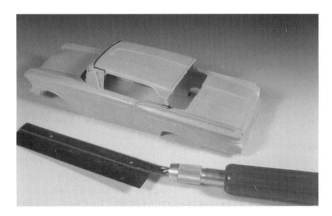

Using a razor saw, carefully remove the hardtop from the Model-haus '57 Mercury to make a convertible. The kit comes with a complete interior. The major change to make here is to remove the right half of the front seat back as marked here in black.

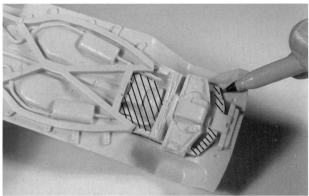

To achieve a steering front suspension, remove the molded-in portion of the frame and front suspension, including the engine and transmission, from the resin chassis. Replace this assembly with the corresponding pieces from the Ertl/AMT 1957 Ford plastic kit.

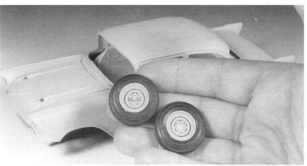

Carl Rees's 1957 Chevrolet "Black Widow" built as a curbside model uses a resin conversion kit from All-American models and parts from an Ertl/AMT '57 Chevrolet Bel Air.

An important part of the final appearance of this '57 Chevy stocker is the correct wheels and tires. The correct six-lug wheels are included in the resin conversion kit. These Firestone tires are available cast in black resin from the Modelhaus. The vinyl tires found in the plastic kit can also be used on the race version.

bench seat, steering column, and steering wheel. You could take a fuel-injected 283 cid small black engine from the Ertl/AMT '57 or '63 Corvette plastic kit.

Remember to wash or soak the resin part thoroughly in a strong household cleaner before attempting any body work, priming, or painting.

Much of the modification has been completed in the interior, including the removal of the rear seat and the reconfiguring of the door panel trim. You'll have to remove the passenger's-side seat back and add a driver's-side bolster made from 1/8″ rod.

Paint the interior tub and the top surface of the dashboard flat black. Paint the front of the dash and steering column metallic gray. Next, photocopy and trim out the seat and side panel fabric pattern provided here. Once the interior paint is thoroughly dry, glue the pieces in place on the seat

and side panels. Spray cement will work best here.

Paint the body shell Testor's Model Master gloss black and white. Cover the body trim, side molding and window trim with Bare-Metal Chrome foil. Once the vacuum-formed windows are trimmed to size, attach them inside the window openings with Sobo white craft glue.

Paint the chassis flat black. Attach the Ertl/AMT kit suspension pieces front and rear. Paint these parts gloss and semigloss black to contrast with the flat finish of the chassis. Add an extra shock absorber to each side of the front and rear suspension. Form exhaust dump pipes from 3/32″ tubing or solid-core solder. Route the dumps from the headers around and out the underside of the car just ahead of the rear wheels. Paint the six-lug wheels gloss white, and remember to highlight the lug nuts on each wheel with

Testor's steel bottle paint applied with a small-diameter brush. Use a set of Firestone "Darlington" tires cast in black resin from the Modelhaus.

After the Corvette engine is assembled, paint the block, cylinder heads, and intake manifold Testor's Chevrolet Engine Red. Paint the fuel injection system components varying shades of aluminum. This is easy to do by mixing in a few drops of flat white with the aluminum to achieve a bit of contrast between the individual parts. Use the headers that are part of the Ertl/AMT '57 plastic kit and brush-paint them with Testor's Jet Exhaust bottle paint.

Currently Fred Cady Design is the only aftermarket decal manufacturer to offer a specific sheet for the "Black Widow" race cars. The Jack Smith no. 47 sheet includes all of the numbers, names, and sponsors needed to compete this vintage stock car model.

3

BOWTIE BRIGADE

BUILDING AND DETAILING A 1962 BEL AIR AND '63 IMPALA NASCAR CHEVROLET

Kenny Collins's '62 Ned Jarrett Chevy Bel Air stock car. He made the head- and taillight covers by using a paper hole punch to make small circles from .010 sheet aluminum.

By 1960 Chevrolet was starting to get its act together. They had not been a serious competitive threat since the '57 season, when Buck Baker took the championship for the marque. Junior Johnson recorded a surprise victory in the '60 Daytona 500 in a year-old Biscayne. Rex White proved that consistency is what counts, winning the championship in a 1960 Impala.

Ned Jarrett is credited with the 1961 Grand National championship driving a Chevy, though he competed part of the season in a Ford. In 1962, Jarrett returned to the series to defend his title in a new Bel Air hardtop looking virtually identical to his '61 championship race car.

The '63 season opened with the most serious effort mounted by Chevrolet to date. Abandoning the old 348/409 cid heavy-duty truck engine used since 1958, Chevy descended on Daytona International Speedway with the Mark Four stagger-valve V-8 engine commonly referred to as the Mystery 427. The highly advanced engine, a forerunner of the division's mid-'60s 396/427 big-block production power plants, was wickedly fast but lacked the durability of the Fords and Pontiacs. Chevrolet withdrew early in the '63 season, leaving the factory teams struggling with few parts and little "support." Chevrolet would not return with a factory effort to the series again until 1971.

Representing this important era in Chevrolet's involvement in NASCAR are two models, the Ned Jarrett '62 Bel Air built by Kenny Collins and the '63 Johnny Rutherford '63 Chevy built by Tim Kolankiewicz. Though built by different modelers, one in Ohio and the other in Alabama, the two models share many kit parts and building techniques.

You will need the following items for the '62 Bel Air:
• Ertl/AMT 1962 Bel Air kit
• Model Car World paint: Silver Blue Metallic and gloss white lacquers
• Tires from the Modelhaus
• Bare-Metal foil
• Decal sheet: no. 638 by Fred Cady Design

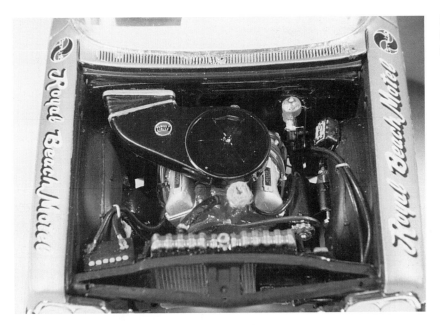

Fig. 3-2. A well-equipped 409 cid stock car engine. Note the full complement of electrical and fluid line plumbing.

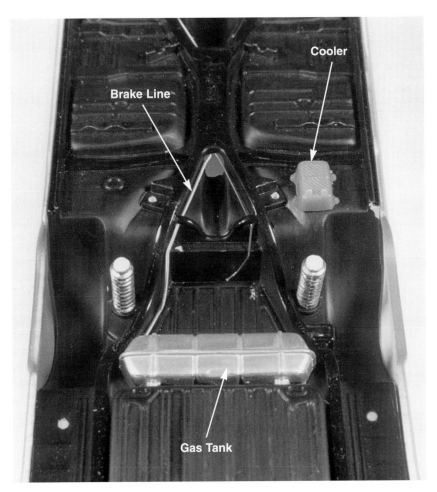

Cooler

Brake Line

Gas Tank

Fig. 3-3. The Ertl/AMT Bel Air chassis is free of extraneous flash or ejector pin marks, meaning virtually no cleanup before painting. Spray the whole chassis bottom surface with Testor's flat black paint. Once the flat finish is thoroughly dry, brush-paint the frame components with gloss black bottle paint. Paint the gas tank with Testor's Metalizer Titanium and the mounting straps aluminum. Note here that brake and fuel lines are added to the chassis. Make the rear brake line using wound guitar string, like that shown here on the left. Again use a length of guitar string, this time the non-wound variety, to represent the gas line (on the right) running from the fuel pump on the engine to the tank in the extreme rear of the chassis. Paint the rear coil springs flat black and glue them in place. As a final touch, use silver bottle paint and a small brush to carefully bring out the raised spring detail by just hitting the high spots with the paint. Add the rear-end cooler and drill two holes for the plumbing.

Fig. 3-4. Assemble the top and bottom halves of the rear axle and paint the assembly gloss black. Add a rear-end pump made from thin sheet plastic and a short length of plastic rod. Paint these parts aluminum and steel. Plumb the rear axle by drilling a pair of holes into the back of the differential. Use two lengths of .050 vinyl-clad wire to represent the coated fluid lines that connect the differential to the cooler with one line passing through the pump.

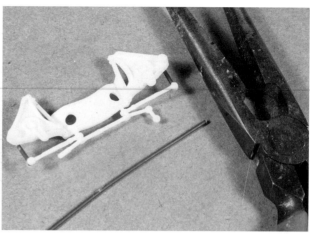

Fig. 3-5. The front suspension will need a bit more attention. Add the right and left steering arms to the tie rod ends, using .060-diameter plastic rod. Crimp one end of each length of rod and glue into place. Paint the assembly gloss black.

Fig. 3-6. To achieve the desired ride height for this vintage stock car, some modifications will be required to the front spindles. First, slice off the raised mounting hole on the kit spindle. Drill a new hole in the face of the spindle below the original hole. Reglue the mounting hole and paint this assembly gloss black.

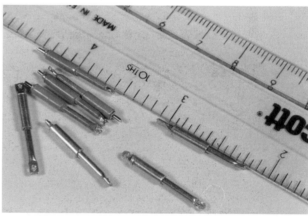

Fig. 3-7. Construct eight shock absorbers from 1/16″ and .095 aluminum tubing. First, cut the two diameters of tubing to length. Then slide the larger-diameter tubing onto the smaller-diameter pieces. Crimp each end of the lengths of 1/16″ tubing. Then drill a .035″ hole in each crimped end. Next file each crimped end into a circular shape. The front shocks are 1 1/32″ end to end. The rear shocks are 15/16″ end to end. Paint each shock absorber and attach in place to the front and rear suspension. Use short lengths of .032 brass rod to make mounting pins for each shock.

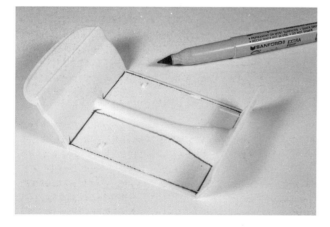

Fig. 3-8. Remove the interior floor, cutting along the lines marked on the kit piece.

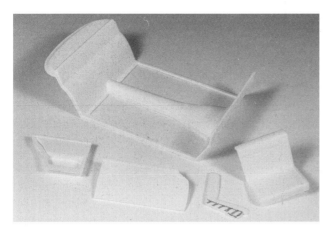

Fig. 3-9. With the interior floor modified as shown, the interior side panels and front seat will need attention. If you choose to represent a bucket seat, use a razor saw to cut the front seat in two. Slice off the end section of the right side of the front seat and reattach it to the side of the new driver's seat.

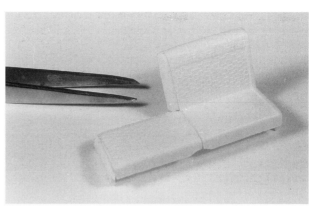

Fig. 3-10. If a bench seat is your choice, remove only the back section of the passenger's side of the front seat. Carefully remove the end section of the seat back and reattach it to the open side of the driver's seat back.

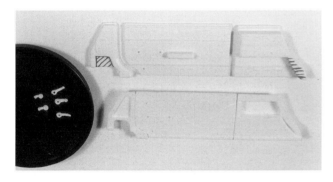

Fig. 3-11. Next, separate the kit side panels into three sections, cutting along the molded-in vertical door lines. This will provide new interior panel lines when the kit pieces are turned inside out to form the stripped-down race car interior sides. Shown here on the bottom is the kit interior panel. Grind away material from the shaded areas. Next drill a series of .035" holes through the base of each piece of door hardware clear through the interior panel. Carefully slice off each door handle and window crank from the surface of the interior panels. On top is a reversed side panel. Note the holes drilled earlier. Note the salvaged door hardware to the right. Take time to test-fit the modified interior, including the revised interior door panels. Better to discover something that doesn't fit quite right at this point in the construction than during final assembly when it might be difficult to fix.

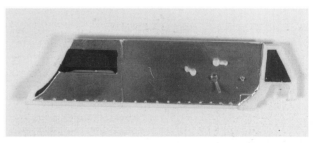

Fig. 3-12. Cover both door panels with Bare-Metal matte finish silver foil. Then, insert short lengths of .030 wire into each hole drilled earlier and remount the door hardware onto the door panel surface. Press the tip of the .030" drill bit into the edge of the foil every 1/16" to represent scale pop rivets.

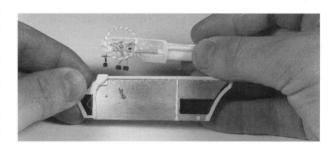

Fig. 3-13. The dashboard with steering column and wheel attached is shown with the finished interior panel. Since the Ertl/AMT kit already represents a stripped-down race car, the dash needs very little attention. Remove the scripts and emblems and drill out the accessory knobs. Wrap the steering wheel with a strip of 1/32" tape to represent the length of fan belt that was wrapped around the steering wheel with electrical tape on the full-size race car.

Fig. 3-14. Temporarily assemble the Blue Ridge roll cage kit and test-fit it into the interior. Narrow the side-to-side width of the cage ¼″ and add ³⁄₃₂″ to the length of the upright bars at the bottom of each one. There should only be one horizontal side bar on each side. Bend each side bar slightly about ⁵⁄₁₆″ in from either end before gluing it into place. Paint the interior panels, bench seat, and floor areas flat white. Paint the seat fabric insert body color.

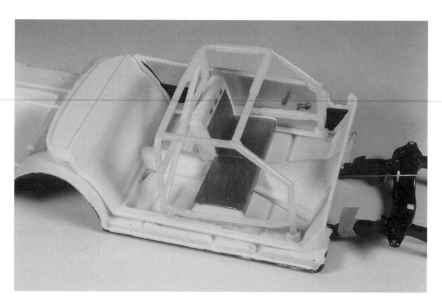

Fig. 3-15. Assemble the Ertl/AMT 409 cid engine according to the kit instructions. The kit comes with a two-four barrel carb manifold. Use a small rectangle of .010 sheet plastic as a cover over the two openings, then mount a single carburetor in the middle. Paint the engine Testor's Chevy Engine Red, the valve covers silver, the transmission aluminum and the cast iron headers Jet Exhaust. Paint the engine accessories like the fan belt flat black and the pulleys, fan blade, and so on, gloss black.

Fig. 3-16. Paint the kit core support and radiator gloss black. Paint the top tank of the radiator with chrome silver. When that's dry, brush on a coating of Tamiya transparent yellow to give the appearance of copper. Note the battery is located on the passenger side of the engine compartment. Mount the engine oil cooler on the front side of the core support behind the left side of the grille.

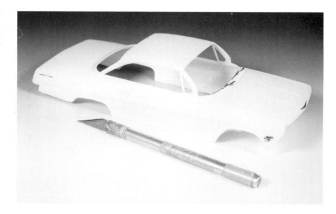

Fig. 3-17. The body shell and hood need little modification except for removing scripts, nameplates, and the windshield wipers along the top edge of the cowling. Take care to work carefully here—you'll have to retain the cowl vent detail.

Fig. 3-18. Chevrolet used six-lug truck hubs and wheels on their race cars until 1963. Use a small ball-shaped grinding bit to grind away the molded-in five-lug bolt head detail around the center of each kit wheel. Work cautiously, being careful to maintain the center hole and stamped shoulder in each wheel. Mark off the wheel center in six equal parts with a soft lead pencil or marker. Next cut equal lengths of .050-diameter plastic rod. Glue each length of rod into place. Spray the wheel with a generous coat of flat white. Then use chrome silver to detail each new lug nut and aluminum to highlight the wheel center detail. A typical front wheel is on the left (grease cap center) while a typical rear wheel (no grease cap) is on the right.

The 1962–63 NASCAR Chevys hark back to an era when stock cars were based on production equipment with slight refinements for safety and, of course, improvements for speed.

1963 NASCAR Chevrolet Impala

To build a '63 Impala stock car model start with the following:

• Ertl/AMT: 1963 Impala kit
• Engine from Revell '69 Yenko Camaro kit
• Model Car World Paint: Smoky Gold and gloss black lacquers
• Decal sheet: no. 628 by Fred Cady Design

The model

Tim Kolankiewicz built this '63 Impala to represent the Chevy pre-pared by legendary Smokey Yunick and driven by Indy veteran Johnny Rutherford in the 1963 Daytona 500. The actual race car was equipped with one of only five of the famous 427 cid "mystery motors." Of the five such cars entered in the race this is the only one to finish.

Tim started with the body, hood, bumpers, and grille from an Ertl/AMT

Fig. 3-19. Tim Kolankiewicz's 1963 NASCAR Impala with the hood open. Note the realistic appearance of the photoetched hood hinges, the Bare-Metal chrome foil treatment around the windows, and the absence of side trim, script, and emblems from the body sides. Tim's treatment of this '63 Chevy chassis is a lesson in subtleties. The careful use of metallic paint shades against the flat black platform is quite effective.

Fig. 3-20. A 1962 Pontiac Catalina built by Dave Dodge from a MCW resin kit. Much of what has been covered here with the '62–'63 Chevys readily applies to this short-wheelbase Pontiac. The paint is from MCW world and the decals are by BSR.

1963 Chevrolet Impala. The remainder of the parts came from the Ertl/AMT '62 Bel Air kit with the engine taken from Revell's Yenko Camaro kit. Some of the parts came from the aftermarket and a few were scratchbuilt. Tim removed the body trim and scratchbuilt bumper inserts along with window frames and reinforcements. The chassis is mostly made up of kit parts from the '62 Bel Air.

The heart of this race car replica is the Mark II big-block engine found in the Revell Yenko Camaro. This engine is the granddaddy of the production 396-427-454 V-8 engine found in full-size Chevrolets from the mid-'60s through the late '70s. External changes included use of two right-side valve covers with fabric to represent the cotton socks used as air cleaner elements and a deep sump oil pan built from scratch. The exotic two-piece exhaust headers were hand-formed from solder wire and plastic tubing.

The interior of this '63 comes straight out of the Ertl/AMT '62 Bel Air with considerable modifications for racing. The bucket seat, steering wheel, and dashboard came from the '63 Impala kit. The model features scratchbuilt door panels, heat-proof asbestos floor covering, roll cage, and shifter. Tim used photoetched items on the interior, including door handles and window cranks, gauge bezels, seat belt hardware, and fasteners.

Tim coated the body, interior pieces, and chassis with automotive primer first. Then, he painted the body with MCW's Smoky Gold and black lacquers. The decals came from Fred Cady design. The wheels, tires, and backing plates are products of Scale Speed Shop.

FASTBACK FORDS AND MERCS

BUILDING AND DETAILING A PLASTIC KIT-BASED '63½ FORD AND '64 MERCURY AND A '64 FORD GALAXIE RESIN KIT

From any view this 1964 Mercury stock car reflects the subtle modifications made to it from the stock kit.

By the early stages of the '63 season, Ford Motor Company was beginning to emerge as the manufacturer fielding the race cars to beat week in and week out in NASCAR. Pontiac and, for the most part, Chevrolet were in the process of going away. Pontiac's last gasp for many years (and it was a good one) was Joe Weatherly, driving for eight different teams, winning the '63 championship. After an explosive debut of its hot new engine at the Daytona 500, Chevrolet quickly backed away from factory support, leaving those teams for the rest of the '63 season with a handful of replacement parts and little else. Chevrolet would not return until 1971. Pontiac did not return until the early 1980s.

The '63 and '64 Fords and Mercurys marked the end of a chassis and suspension design that had served the corporation's cars quite well, on the street and on the racetrack, since they were introduced in 1957. Though Ford race cars would adopt a totally new perimeter-type frame in 1965, the '63 and '64 race cars from the company's sister divisions set quite a pace on the racetrack.

Fortunately for the stock car modeler, the Ertl company continues to reissue two of the stalwarts of that important era in motor sports. Plastic 1/25 scale kits of the 1963½ Galaxie and 1964 Mercury Marauder are readily available at hobby shops, discount stores, or swap meets.

Unlike the purpose-built race car kits that we are all so familiar with today, these great old kits will need much TLC to render a true and accurate replica of those factory race cars driven by the likes of Ned Jarrett, Darrell Derringer, Marvin Panch, Dan Gurney, Fred Lorenzen, Curtis Turner, and Fireball Roberts.

Seen here are two such race cars, the handiwork of Daryl Huhtala. We will show you how to convert a street-stock production kit into a fire-breathing 160 mph stock car. By contrast, you will also see how to build a 1964 Ford Galaxie using a purpose-manufactured resin kit from the Modelhaus. In the resin kit, most of the really time-consuming and painstaking conversion work has been already completed.

You will need the following items for the plastic kit conversions:

• Ertl/AMT 1963½ Ford Galaxie hardtop or 1964 Mercury Marauder hardtop, 1966 Fairlane, 1957 Ford Fairlane

  • Testor's bottle and spray paints
  • your choice of decals

• sheet plastic, solder wire, etc.
• Modelhaus resin wheels and tires
• Preston's prewired distributor
• Detail Resources wire loom, interior details
• Detail Master battery hardware, engine detailing set no. 1

Many of these items are available from a single source, BSR Replicas and Finishes. Grab your kits, tools, and paint and join us now as we present two approaches to building pieces of racing history.

Chassis

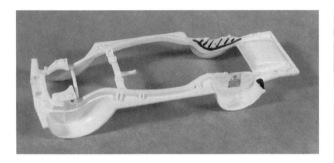

Fig. 4-2. Remove not only the floor pan between the frame rails as shown, but also trim away all the floor pan between the frame rails from the transmission support to the fuel tank. Then remove the molded-on rear suspension, which includes the rear springs.

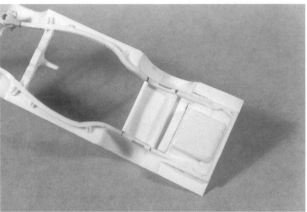

Fig. 4-3. Use .020 sheet plastic to replace the trunk floor outside the frame rails behind the rear wheel wells. Then add the two frame cross braces at the rear axle, using ⅛˝ aluminum welding rod. The forward brace is bent upward slightly in a V shape, providing proper clearance for the driveshaft. Add .020 sheet plastic from the gas tank to the forward brace on top of the frame to close off this area.

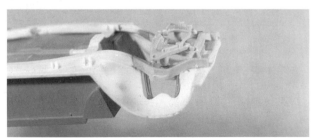

Figs. 4-4 and 4-5. Next, remove the front frame rails and upper suspension components forward of the firewall. In like fashion remove the corresponding assembly from the chassis of an AMT '57 Ford. This conversion now equips your model with a steering front suspension.

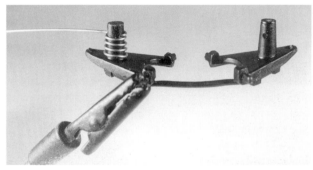

Fig. 4-6. You can enhance the front suspension detail further by using .025 solder wire. Wrap a length around the spring section to form coil springs. Six or seven turns should be enough to make them look realistic.

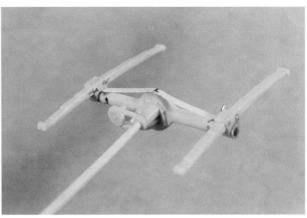

Figs. 4-7 and 4-8. Now adapt the rear axle and leaf springs from an AMT '66 Fairlane to use in place of those molded-in parts you removed earlier. Add 1/8″ pieces of 1/8″-diameter aluminum tubing to each end of the axle housing. This will increase the overall width of the rear axle to that of the original Galaxie unit. Then

drill .025″ holes through the springs and insert short lengths of .022 solder wire to serve as the new mounting pins for the rear shock absorbers. Use a length of .020 sheet plastic to make an axle stiffener and glue into place.

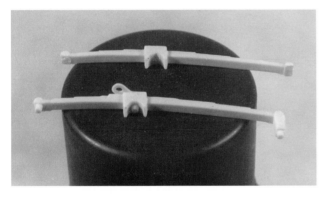

Fig. 4-9. Cut off the molded-on shock absorber mounting pins, then glue them in place on the axle so they line up with the spring mounts and aft frame rails. Also remove the four mounting pins from either end of each leaf spring. Construct four rear shock absorbers, using lengths of 1/16″-diameter aluminum tubing and heat-shrink tubing, as shown in the diagram.

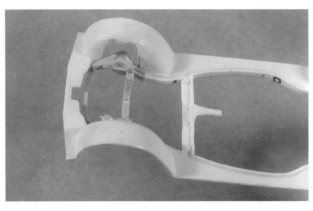

Fig. 4-10. Trim away the front inner fender panels to provide adequate clearance for the dual shocks on both front sides of the suspension.

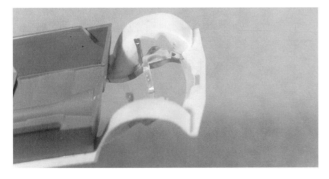

Fig. 4-11. Drill two .090″ holes in each front frame rail to mount the shock towers. Make two of these from 3/32″ aluminum tubing cut to length. Next, flatten a small portion of the top end of each tower with needle-nose pliers and then drill a .030″ hole to attach to each front shock.

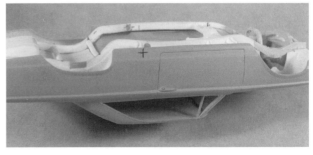

Fig. 4-12. At this point, returning to the center area of the chassis, drill two 5/32″ holes through the side frame rails. These openings should be large enough to allow 5/32″ tubing to pass completely through.

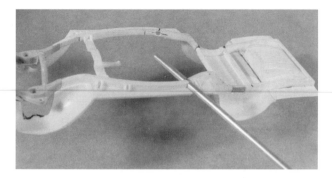

Fig. 4-13. Make sure the holes are not too large in diameter—there should be a nice snug fit when the dump pipes are in place. You also need to cut away a small portion of the lower edge of the quarter panel where the exhaust dump will eventually exit. Cut two small reinforcing gusset plates from .020 sheet plastic and glue them in place over the area where the exhaust dumps pass through the frame rails.

Fig. 4-14. Coat the entire chassis with primer. Then paint the chassis surface with Testor's Model Master flat black. When dry, give the surface a light dusting of semigloss clear as a final coat.

Interior

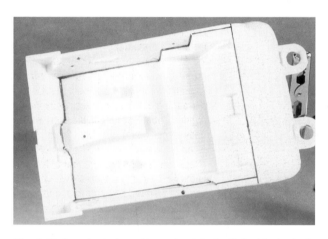

Fig. 4-15. In order to have the racing interior fit inside the body as the stock one did, first cut the rear package shelf at its leading edge and remove it from the back of the interior bucket. Next, remove the rear seat and rear seat armrests, making the cut where they meet the side panels at the interior floor.

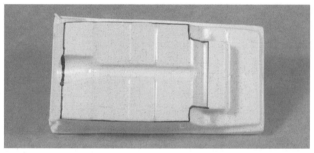

Fig. 4-16. Carefully cut away the bottom horizontal area of the interior floor with a razor saw. Replace this portion of the racing interior with a vacuum-formed copy of the interior floor from the Dukes of Hazard Charger kit (or a suitable substitute featuring a smooth surface). Glue the new floor in place. Use two small pieces of .020 sheet plastic as shims at the aft ends of the side panels to replace plastic removed by the width of the saw cut. Fill the remaining gaps in the rear of the interior tub with .010 sheet plastic.

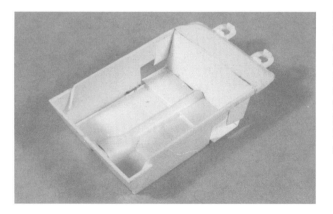

Fig. 4-17. Then reposition the stock rear package shelf back in its original location. Next, sand smooth the surface of both right and left interior panels and then drill .025″ holes in the side panels where the window cranks were originally located. Make a paper template of the clean side panel. Trim out new side panels for both sides of the interior from .010 sheet plastic, taking that shape from the template. Wait to install them in a later step. So far, you have gutted the new racing interior to resemble a racing stock car. For this application it is now the same size and shape as the original kit interior. Test-fitting proves this point.

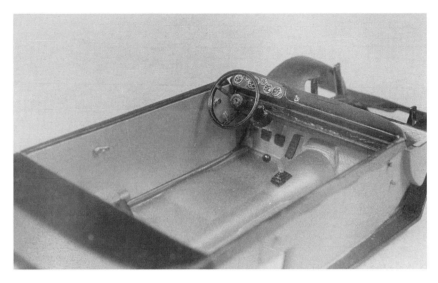

Fig. 4-18. Paint the floor and rear walls of the interior light gray with a very light mist coat of silver to simulate the gray speckle finish that was common for some cars of this era. Paint the separate side panels made earlier from sheet stock with Testor's Metalizer Aluminum and when thoroughly dry buff with a soft cloth to a shine. Then glue the panels into place. Window cranks were still required in these cars, as side glass was required for the larger speedways. Use the holes made earlier in the side panels as a guide and drill final mounting holes for door glass and quarter window crank handles. Follow the diagram provided to construct the handles.

Fig. 4-19. Use the stock driver's seat from the Ertl/AMT kit and add a side bolster made from 1/8" solder wire. Paint the seat Testor's flat black. After painting the seat, add a set of five-point seat belts like those from Detail Master. To convert the stock kit dash layout to a racing configuration, grind away all the production details. Replace the stock instrument cluster with a grouping of racing gauges. Once they're painted, add instrument faces from Fred Cady decal sheet no. 183. Simulate the clear lenses over the instrument faces by simply mixing a small amount of two-part epoxy and flowing a drop or two into each housing. When it's dry, the epoxy will have leveled out and will remain clear as glass. Use the kit steering wheel. Remove the horn ring and paint the wheel and column black.

Fig. 4-20. Many materials are suitable for constructing an accurate roll cage. Here 1/8" aluminum welding rod, 3/32" aluminum tubing, and electrical shrink tube for the padding are used.

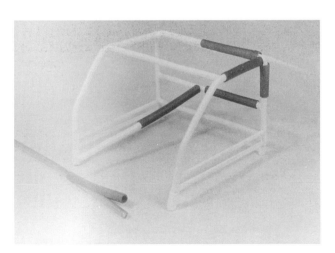

Fig. 4-21. Glue the Galaxie kit engine block and transmission halves together. Fill the slot or gap in the oil pan with pieces of sheet plastic. Other parts to add to the engine assembly include the carb and manifold from a late model Ertl/AMT stock car kit and the valve covers and coil from their 427 Fairlane kit engine. Drill .015″ holes for spark plug wires next, along with 1/16″ holes for exhaust headers at each exhaust port. To make individual headers from solder wire, cut four 4″ lengths of 1/16″ solid-core solder. Insert the end of each piece of solder into one of the four holes on each side of the engine. Temporarily install the engine into the chassis and begin bending each length of solder back and down, making sure to clear all bracing and suspension components. Once all four lengths have been formed into a bundle, cut the bundle to length just below the transmission support.

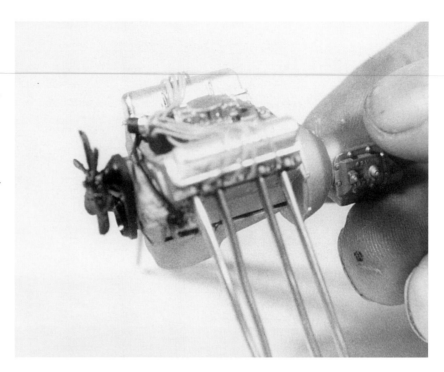

Fig. 4-22. Cut two 1/4″ lengths of 3/16″ aluminum tubing, which you will slide over the ends of both bundles to form a collector. First, though, cut four short lengths of 1/16″ brass rod and form into a bundle resembling the solder wires. Then insert this assembly into the aluminum tubing and use it as a die. With the aid of a flat-end screwdriver carefully press the aluminum in and around the bundle. Remove the brass rod and slip the new collector over the ends of each bundle of solder wire headers.

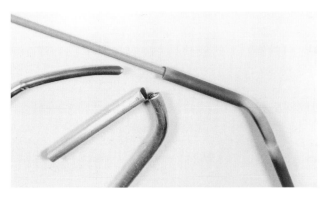

Figs. 4-23, 4-24. Form the exhaust dump pipes by inserting a piece of 3/32″ solder wire into a length of 5/32″ aluminum tubing. Bend the tubing to the desired angle and cut it to the proper length. This procedure can also be used with plastic tubing and plastic rod. The objective here is to achieve a uniform bend without distorting or collapsing the tubing walls.

Fig. 4-25. Finish the engine up by painting the block gunmetal, the transmission aluminum, the heads and intake aluminum, and the valve covers silver. Detail the engine and engine bay further, adding the battery, coil, voltage regulator, and solenoid, and the remaining parts of the ignition system.

Wheels and tires

Fig. 4-26. The distinctive Holman-Moody–style five-lug wheels are resin and come from the Modelhaus. Remove the spindle ends that protrude through the rear wheel centers with a ball-shaped bit. The tires are also resin and from Modelhaus. After washing away the mold release, paint the wheels light blue, adding wheel weights and valve stems. The "Firestone" tire lettering is actually a water-slide decal available on the no. 183 decal sheet from Fred Cady Design.

Body shell

Fig. 4-27. Remove most of the chrome trim from the lower body. This includes fender ornaments, windshield wipers, badging, scripting, and all other ornamentation except the door handles. Leave them intact. Once the initial operation is completed, use medium- and fine-grit sandpapers along with an emery board to clean up and smooth out the areas affected. Follow this with a few light coats of automotive sandable primer like Plasticote T-235. Repeatedly sanding the areas where the trim is removed after applying primer will help you see imperfections.

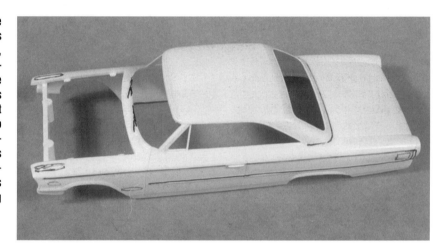

Fig. 4-28. Use a ball-type grinding bit to remove the grille emblem and script from the front bumper and grille, along with the molded-in headlight lenses. Then, using a single-hole paper punch, cut small disks from .010 sheet plastic to make covers for the head- and taillight openings. Paint them aluminum.

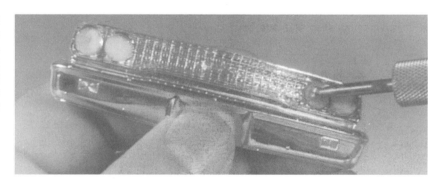

Fig. 4-29. At the rear, separate the rear taillight and trim panel from the rear bumper. Cover the hatched trim area between the taillight bezels with a piece of .010 sheet plastic. Cut a U-shaped opening in the lower center of the panel for the gas filler neck. Clean the area up to a smooth finish, prime and paint body color.

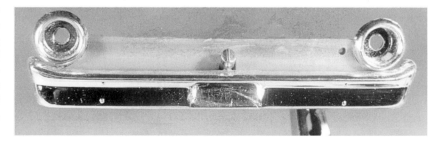

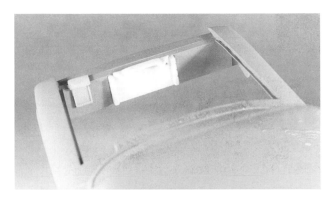

Fig. 4-30. Smooth out the core support by grinding away the chassis mounting towers. Then paint the resin oil cooler aluminum and mount it in place along with the kit radiator.

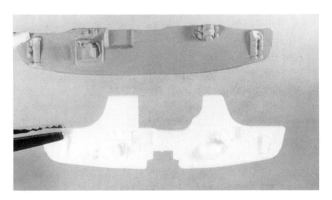

Fig. 4-31. Remove all the unnecessary accessories from the face of the firewall. Be sure to leave the brake master cylinder. The lower edges of the kit firewall leave noticeable gaps between the interior tub and the edge of the chassis on either side of the transmission. Trim off the bottom of the firewall as shown. Finally, fill in the hood spring clip notch in the top center of the firewall with a piece of sheet plastic. Coat the entire body shell with a good-quality automotive primer and sand to a smooth finish, then paint it shell white. Krylon white lacquer was used here. Then, mask off the roof area and paint the lower portion of the body shell in a very light pale gray-blue. To match this Ford factory color, mix ¼ ounce of Testor's gloss white with 12 drops of no. 8 blue and 6 drops of gloss black. Stir thoroughly and thin to one part paint to one part thinner. Apply with an airbrush. Remove the masking and allow about two full weeks for the finish to cure. Rub out the body shell surface using a professional polishing kit like the one from Micro-Mesh. Use Bare-Metal foil to highlight the trim around the windows and the door handles. Apply the adhesive-backed foil generously. Rub it down to conform to the various contours with a tissue and cotton swab. Then trim away the excess with a fresh X-Acto blade. The markings for this Ford were originally produced by JNJ Hobbies and may still be available from BSR Replicas and Finishes. There are numerous other decal sheets that will make a pleasing subject.

Fig. 4-32. Don't forget to apply a flat black wash to the grille to bring out the recessed details. Three hood pins are mandated to hold the closed hood in place in case the latch should be jarred loose. Note the sheet plastic pieces used to cover the turn signals in the bumper.

Fig. 4-33. Use the Detail Master photoetched hood pin set no. 2320 to make the assemblies for the rear deck lid. Note here the plastic disks substituted for the stock taillight lenses. The fuel overflow tube on the right is made from a short length of ¹⁄₁₆˝ aluminum tubing. Make two safety straps to hold the rear window in place at high speed

Fig. 4-34. Automotive electrical and plumbing diameters

Part	1/24–1/25 scale
Plug wires	.013˝
Fuel lines	.020˝
Oil lines	.040˝
Radiator	.80˝
Brake lines	.010˝

5

HEMI REIGNS!

BUILDING AND DETAILING HEMI V-8 '64 DODGES AND PLYMOUTHS

This '64 Dodge and Plymouth use similar graphics and look as if they could be team cars. The Dodge is built by kitbashing a Jo-Han Dodge with an Ertl/AMT '68 Road Runner. The Plymouth is built from a Jo-Han kit with modifications accomplished the old-fashioned way!

The 1964 NASCAR Grand National season marked the year Chrysler Corporation finally climbed back to the top of the mountain. Not since Carl Kiekhaefer's Chrysler 300s dominated the '55 and '56 season had this company enjoyed such great success in motorsports. A brand-new Hemi V-8 engine was the reason. The mighty power plant had been in secret development since late 1962. The hemispherical-head 426 cid engine with a dual overhead valve combustion chamber gave Chrysler an awesome weapon in the battle for racing supremacy. In late 1963, word had leaked out that tests under near-

racing conditions had yielded lap speeds exceeding 185 mph! Remember, the competition, namely Ford Galaxies and Mercury Marauders, were turning practice laps at Daytona of only 165 mph!

In the race, Richard Petty dominated, leading a parade of Plymouths and Dodges in a 1-2-3 finish to take the checkered flag and win the 1964 Daytona 500. Eight Hemi-equipped Mopars started the race—four Dodges and four Plymouths. It was Richard Petty's first super speedway win and the first of what would prove to be seven such victories in this prestigious event.

Presented here are two of the

Hemi-powered cars that competed in the '64 Daytona 500. Jimmy Pardue's no. 54 Plymouth was a close second to Richard Petty's no. 43 Plymouth. The David Pearson no. 6 Dodge crashed and did not finish the race.

Two contrasting approaches to building these stock-based race cars are covered in this chapter. As you will soon discover, one method makes the racing conversion to the basic kit, and the other makes those modifications by the kitbashing method.

The Plymouth is a converted 1/25 Jo-Han '64 Plymouth race car kit. Either Jo-Han kit, '64 Dodge or Plymouth, can just barely be called a "race car" model kit. Most of the racing details in these two kits are pretty superficial. By contrast, Daryl Huhtala used a '64 Dodge Jo-Han kit body shell combined with the chassis and running gear from an Ertl-AMT's '68 Road Runner kit. Whatever course you choose, adhering closely to either approach will yield an accurate replica.

Things you will need to get started include:
• Jo-Han 1964 Plymouth kit no. GC 964 or
• Jo-Han 1964 Dodge kit no. GC 2864
• Any one of the various Ertl/AMT Plymouth or Dodge kits, for example, the '68 Road Runner (6515),

'69 GTX, or 1970 Dodge Super Bee
• Fred Cady Design decals
• Plasticote, Spinnaker White for the Pardue Plymouth
• Testor's spray and bottle paints
• Modelhaus resin wheels and tires
• Detail Master photoetched hood pin kit

1964 Dodge

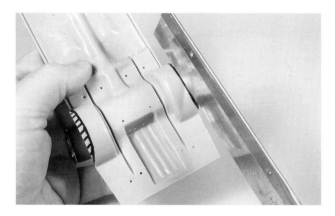

Fig. 5-2. When using the chassis from an Ertl/AMT Plymouth, remove roughly 5/32″ pieces from each of the rear inner fender panels. The Jo-Han '64 Dodge body requires a bit more clearance in this area to make sure the two parts fit properly.

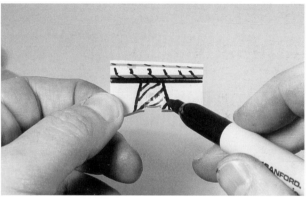

Fig. 5-3. Fortunately, the Ertl/AMT Plymouth kit front inner fender panels are separate pieces. This makes the job of modifying them a great deal easier. Here you need to remove the portions of the panels as marked, to the dimensions shown. Then glue a length of 3/32″ plastic rod to the top of the remaining pieces.

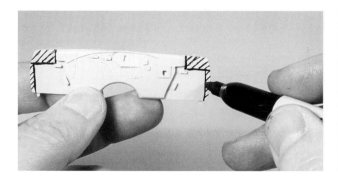

Fig. 5-4. For proper fit and clearance inside the Jo-Han Dodge body shell, notch out both sides of the firewall to the dimensions shown here. Note the alignment pins (there are two on each side of the firewall). The new inner fender panels mount against these pins once the firewall is glued into place on the chassis.

Fig. 5-5. Once the firewall is in place, attach the fender panels into position. Super glue is recommended for this type of work. Note the position of the alignment pins and the rear edge of the inner fender panel.

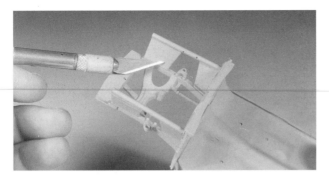

Fig. 5-6. Next drill two .020″ holes in the plastic rod at the corners of the opening in the fender panel. These holes will be used as the top attachment point for the dual front shocks.

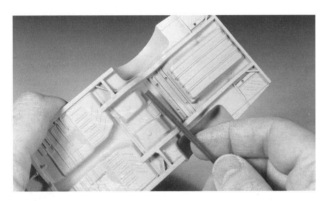

Fig. 5-8. At the rear of the chassis, you'll have to add a second shock mount bracket. Cut a 1″ piece of 1/8″ C-channel and glue it into place 1/4″ forward of the kit bracket.

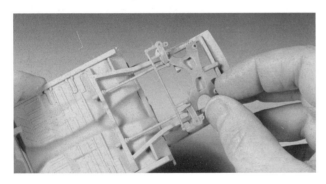

Fig. 5-10. Now that the really hard work has been done on the new chassis, you can set about the task of painting and assembling the other components according to the Ertl/AMT kit instruction sheet.

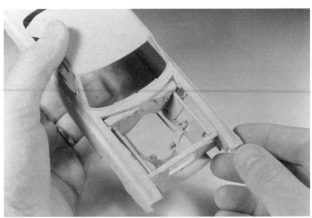

Fig. 5-7. Periodic test-fitting will ensure a proper alignment and trouble-free final assembly. Here you can see that each end of the firewall allows clearance for hood hinges. The horizontal support tubing (made from 3/32″ plastic rod) should touch both the firewall in the rear and the core support at the front of the engine compartment on both sides.

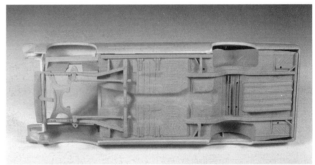

Fig. 5-9. Final inspection of the fit and alignment of the Road Runner chassis reveals that the new parts mate to the Jo-Han Dodge body like the proverbial hand in glove. The precise alignment of the wheel wells in the chassis with the fender openings in the body is most important.

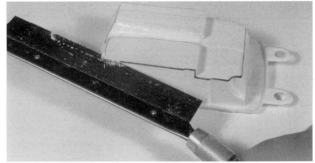

Fig. 5-11. Daryl opted for improved clearance between body, interior, and chassis by slicing off the floor of the Dodge interior. Work carefully with a razor saw for the flat surfaces. After modifications have been made by kitbashing the Jo-Han and Ertl/AMT parts, the remainder of the building process for this 1964 Dodge is very much the same as for the '64 Plymouth.

Fig. 5-12. The Jo-Han chassis has all the surface details molded in. Remove the entire exhaust system using both a cylindrical bit with a flat end and a ball-shaped bit in a motor tool running at a slow speed. Be patient and take care not to damage remaining surface details inadvertently. Once the exhaust system is history, trim away the entire area of the chassis where the mufflers were located. This will require some additional work with the motor tool, as well as hand work with hobby knife, files, and sandpaper.

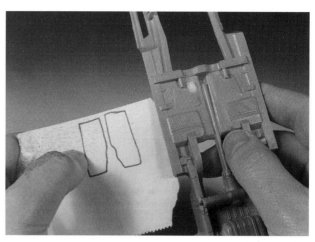

Fig. 5-13. Use a piece of card stock to make a template as depicted here. Then use the template to cut out corresponding shapes from .030 sheet plastic. Next, glue these new pieces of the chassis floor into place.

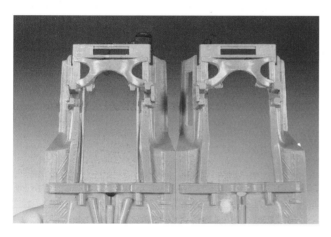

Fig. 5-14. At the front of the kit chassis proceed to trim away the molded-in torsion bars.

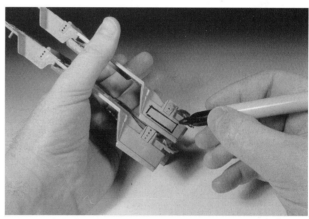

Fig. 5-15. Measure an opening ⅜″ x ⅞″ to be cut in both the right and left inner fender panels. Before you start cutting, mark the dimension with a permanent marker so that the area to be removed is clearly visible.

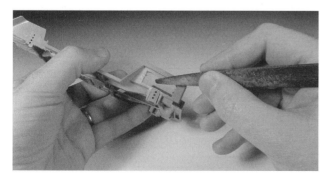

Fig. 5-16. Clean the openings up with a flat file, making sure you keep the edges straight and the corners square.

Fig. 5-17. Using the dimensions provided, build the front suspension. It may look complicated, but being patient and working methodically will yield a realistic assembly. Note the mounting bracket attached to each lower control arm, which is used to attach the dual front shocks to the part of the front suspension that travels. The finished suspension should resemble this configuration. It is now ready for primer and paint.

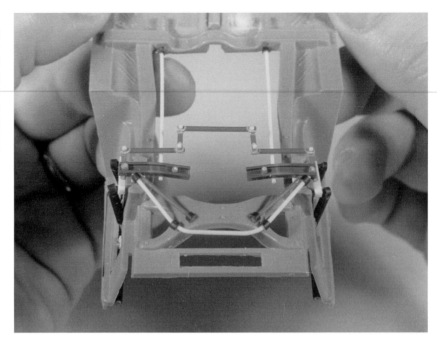

Fig. 5-18. On the top side, add a length of 3/32″ plastic rod horizontally along the top edge of the inner fender panel on both sides of the engine compartment. Attach to pieces of 1/16″ plastic rod fore and aft of the right and left upper control arm. Cut a small square of .030 sheet plastic and glue it into the inside corners. Then drill two corresponding holes and insert short lengths of .025 plastic rod in all four locations. You'll use these pins for the upper fixed attachment of each front shock absorber.

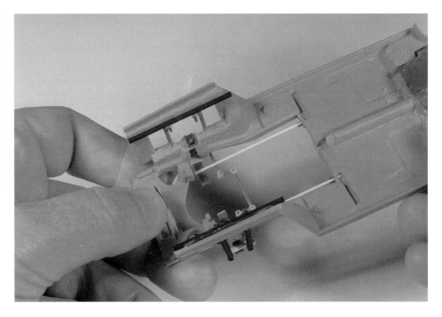

Fig. 5-19

.080 Ring
.040 Rod
.080 Tube
.080 Ring

Typical Shock

$\frac{7}{16}$
$\frac{7}{16}$

Rear Shocks

$\frac{3}{8}$
$\frac{3}{8}$

Lower Control Arm
.040 Rod

Front Shocks

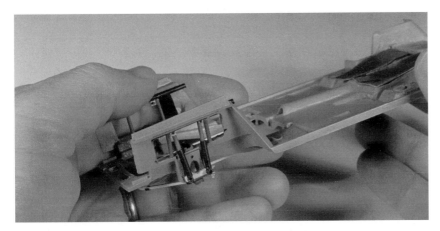

Fig. 5-20. Following fig. 5-19, make four adjustable shocks from plastic tubing and rod. Since the shocks are adjustable, attach one end of each shock absorber and extend or contract it to the proper length. For the rear suspension, construct two mounting brackets and attach them to the ends of the rear axle. Attach each rear shock to the pins on each end of the brackets.

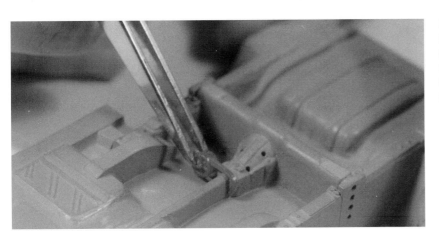

Fig. 5-21. You may choose to add a rear-end cooler. This one is from my scrap box and is similar to ones found in many current stock car kits. Attach it between the snout of the differential and the rear end of the driveshaft.

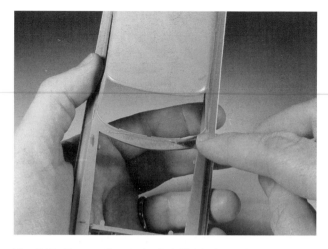

Fig. 5-22. Remove the stock windshield wipers that are molded into the cowling. Using a new X-Acto blade, carefully slice the wiper arm from the horizontal surface. Finish the job with a small file and sandpaper.

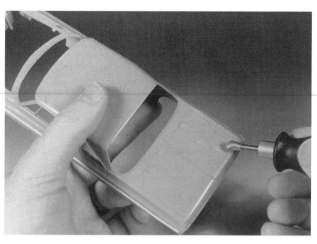

Fig. 5-23. There are a few surface imperfections in both the Plymouth and Dodge bodies. Most are sink marks and can be easily filled with micro-balloons and super glue or Dr. Micro Tool body filler. For best results, carefully rough up the area to be repaired before applying your choice of filler.

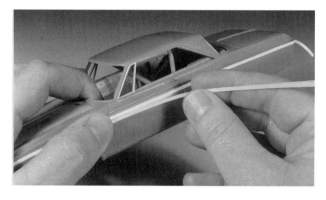

Fig. 5-24. To make the Belvedere side trim, first take a length of 1/16″ automotive stripping tape and run it along the body side panels 1/16″ from the horizontal accent line. Then cut out the side molding from a sheet of .020 sheet plastic. Carefully attach the new trim piece to the body surface, using liquid cement for styrene plastic. This is a slow-drying glue and will allow you the time to work the trim into its proper location.

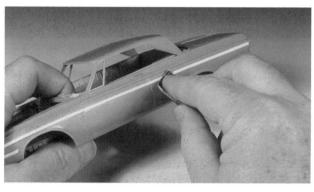

Fig. 5-25. Once the cement is thoroughly dry, work the surface of the side trim to a beveled contour. This will require some patience, and you may wish to use a sanding block or emery board on the long, gradually curved surfaces. When you are satisfied with the shape and contour of the side trim, don't forget to cut the door lines into the sides for both doors.

Fig. 5-26. Make a hood pin panel and attach it in place in front of the core support and just below the inside surface of the hood.

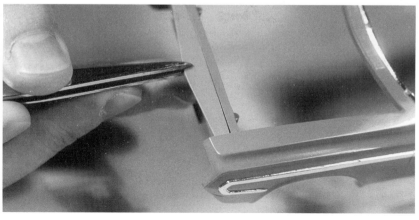

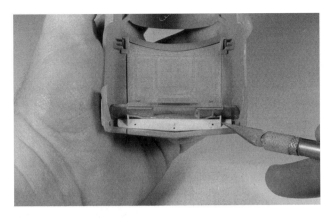

Fig. 5-27. You might want to add a couple of triangular reinforcements on the underside. Next reinstall the hood and drill three .020″ holes through the hood and through the new panel. The rules require five retainer clips for the front windshield for 1964. Make these pieces from .010 sheet plastic and attach. Do this work before applying the final primer and paint to the body.

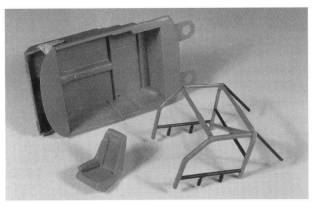

Fig. 5-28. The Jo-Han kit interior already has a removable rear seat and a racing instrument cluster for the dashboard. Add pieces of 3/32″ and 1/16″ plastic rod to the kit roll cage for the no. 6 Dodge and no. 54 Plymouth.

Fig. 5-29. The Pearson Dodge is painted as follows: white exposed panels, red dash, door panels, and bucket seat. Paint the interior of the Pardue Plymouth aluminum on the exposed panels, black for the dash, seat, and door panels. Note the location of the rear-end cooling fan, roll bar padding, and fire extinguisher. Tape all small individual pieces and assemblies to a piece of cardboard using curls of masking tape. Mount the body shell to a hobby paint stand—or you can make one by bending a metal coat hanger to shape. This will allow you to handle these items while painting without the fear of dropping or loosing something in the process.

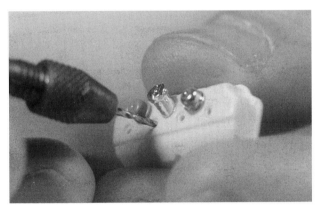

Fig. 5-30. Carefully drill out each spark plug hole in the large valve covers and attach oil filler necks and breathers.

Fig. 5-31. Begin building and detailing the engine by drilling out the center of the distributor cap to accept a bundle of nine lengths of fine wire. Next assemble the basic engine and transmission pieces. Then fill, file, and sand smooth all seams and give this assembly a light coat of primer. Other engine accessories, including the fuel pump, are prepared next for painting. Typical paint colors for these engine were gunmetal for the engine block and cylinder heads, aluminum for the oil pan, chrome silver for the valve covers, and steel for the headers.

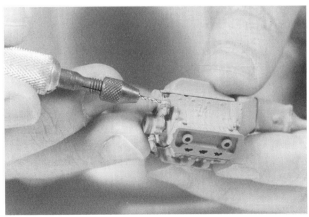

Fig. 5-32. Once the engine is painted the detailing begins in earnest. Note here the fuel line, which originates at the front of the car with the carburetor, passes through the fuel pump, and runs along the chassis to the fuel tank. I generally use uncoated wire approximately .015 to do most of the engine wiring. Once it's in place, then carefully brush-paint the wiring with whatever color or coating is accurate for a particular model. Remember to drape the cables and lines gently to give a real-world and natural look to the finished assembly.

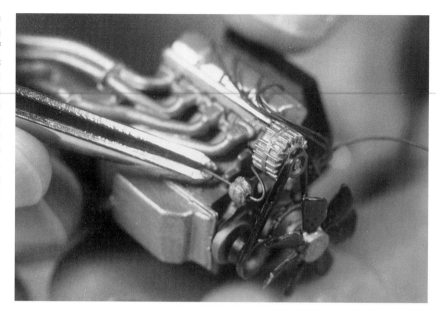

Fig. 5-33. The completed engine compartment should include a detailed battery, oil cooler, racing air cleaner that attaches to the base of the cowling at the firewall, radiator with overflow, and plumbed brake master cylinder. Note here the addition of an optional oil breather tube running between the upper front corners of the valve covers.

Fig. 5-34. After the body shell is painted, install the handmade hood pins and retainer clips. Use a small-diameter brush and paint a small area around each hole in the hood to represent the scuff plates.

Fig. 5-35. Install the sewing needles so enough of the eye protrudes above the surface of the hood for the retainer clip to pass through comfortably. Note the hood pin clips and the silver thread used to attach them to the car. When the glue and paint are dry, close the hood and position each retainer clip through its corresponding needle eye. The finished job should look like this. Run the open ends of the attachment cables to small-diameter holes drilled under the leading edge of the hood.

Fig. 5-36. A wash of flat black cut with thinner and flowed into the recesses of the grille adds to the realism.

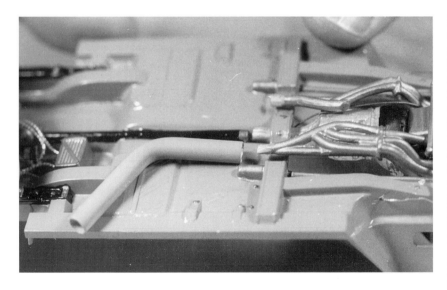

Figs. 5-37 and 5-38. To complete the chassis detail, make a set of exhaust dump pipes from aluminum or plastic tubing bent to shape and slipped over the ends of the headers. Not every race car of the period used the same approach to exhausting the combustion gases. Some teams preferred the dumps to exit with a single pipe from each side of the car. Other teams ran the dump pipes side by side, out one side of the car. Note the reinforcement straps on the Plymouth's gas tank made from 1/16″ strips of tape and painted semigloss black. The rear-end cooler is a resin piece from the Modelhaus. The safety strap for the driveshaft is made from a strip of .020 sheet plastic. Paint the chassis body color. Paint the details of the front and rear chassis components with Testor's flat, semigloss and gloss black, silver, aluminum, gunmetal, steel and Jet Exhaust bottle paints.

6

THE HALF-CHASSIS CAR

BUILDING A '66–'67 FORD FAIRLANE NASCAR STOCKER

The major components to replicate an accurate 1966–67 Ford half-chassis race car are pictured here. With the addition of the proper paint and body markings, many historically significant race cars can be duplicated in miniature.

Ford Motor Company withdrew their factory teams from NASCAR competition after the eighth race of the '66 season at Atlanta Motor Speedway. The refusal by the sanctioning body to allow them to race their monster overhead cam 427 engine in competition and the continued use of the 426 Hemi by Chrysler race cars apparently gave them no alternative.

Chrysler's withdrawal of their factory teams during the devastating 1965 season was not repeated during the '66

campaign. Many Ford and Mercury factory drivers jumped ship, getting rides in any competitive race car just so they could stay employed. The pressure was definitely on Ford, as they were temporarily out of the spotlight and really out of the on-track action.

Late in the season, Bud Moore brought a new '66 Mercury Comet to the racetrack for Darrell Derringer to drive. At first NASCAR inspectors turned the team and their new car away. Obviously there wasn't much that one could call "stock" about these

new stock cars. The street version of the Fairlane and Comet were built with a unibody—the body and chassis were composed of many metal stampings welded together to form a single structure. This was quite a departure from the Galaxie race cars used by the Ford teams earlier in the season, which had a body shell bolted to a perimeter frame.

These new Ford and Mercury race cars were neither fish nor fowl. The entire front snout, upper and lower control arms, dual shock absorber, and so on, from the '65–'66 Galaxie had been attached to the Ford intermediate unibody platform at the firewall. Then hand-fabricated side beams were welded to the new front end, around the outside edge of the production platform, and attached to the rear subframe, effectively tying the whole structure together similarly to a body-over-frame design.

At first NASCAR wanted nothing to do with this new creation. But . . . those empty seats in the grandstands spoke volumes, especially if your normal vocabulary contains a lot of dollar signs! Finally the sanctioning body approved the new concoction, and the reference in the Grand National rule book to race cars being built from production components was gone forever. The hybrid chassis under these '66–'67 Fords and Mercurys, except for the rear suspension, is basically what is found under every NASCAR Ford, Mercury, Chevrolet, Pontiac, Buick, and Oldsmobile race car that followed. Though small improvements and changes have been incorporated for safety reasons, today's NASCAR stock car chassis has virtually been frozen in time for over 30 years. Come along as Randy Derr builds, in miniature, a landmark chassis that set the level of technology for NASCAR racing for over 30 years.

Some of the things you'll need to build a typical half-chassis Ford race car of the late '60s and early '70s:

• Ertl/AMT '66 Ford Fairlane kit
• Monogram Thunderbird stock car
• paint colors of your choice
• decals of your choice (Slixx, Fred Cady, BSR and JNJ have a few decal sheets that allow you some choice in which cars you build)
• resin wheels, tires, and accessory items like oil cooler and cooling fan housings and reservoirs from the Modelhaus
• plastic sheet, rod, and tubing

Randy Derr's building and detailing tips and techniques presented here will work equally well for a '66–'67 Mercury Comet, a '68 through 1971 Ford Torino, and a 1969 Torino Talledega.

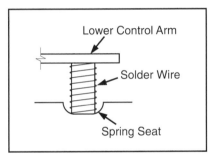

Fig. 6-1

Fig. 6-2. First, remove the front subframe, including the engine and transmission cross members from the Ertl/AMT '65 Galaxie chassis (discard the piece with zebra stripes). Then remove the front subframe from the '66 Fairlane chassis (the part painted black).

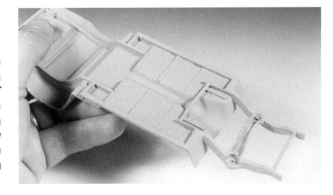

Fig. 6-3. Attach the '65 Galaxie subframe to the front of the '66 unibody platform. Next add two L-shaped frame rails to each side of the Fairlane platform. Make these pieces from 1/16″ x 1/8″ strips of Evergreen plastic bar stock. This effectively ties the front and rear subframe together like the stock chassis from a production '65–'66 Ford Galaxie (fig. 6-4). Also, make a new transmission mount from 1/16″-diameter plastic rod. Prime the new assembly to help identify any areas needing attention with filler or sanding.

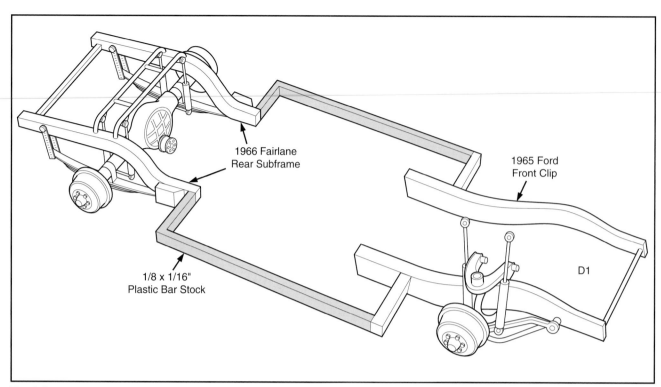

1966 Fairlane
Rear Subframe

1965 Ford
Front Clip

1/8 x 1/16"
Plastic Bar Stock

D1

Fig. 6-4

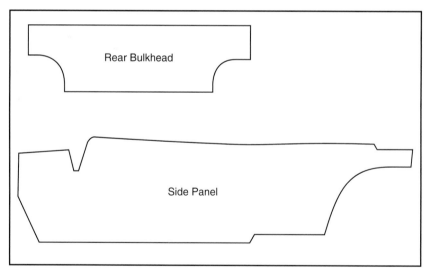

Rear Bulkhead

Side Panel

Fig. 6-5

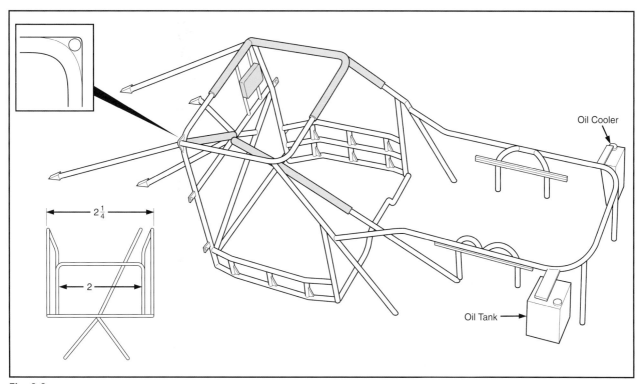

Oil Cooler

$2\frac{1}{4}$

2

Oil Tank

Fig. 6-6

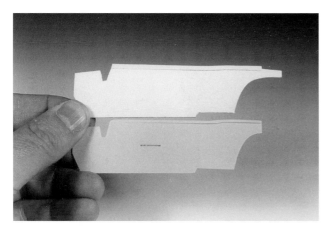

Fig. 6-7. The lower piece pictured here is a Fairlane kit interior side panel. The upper one is a scratchbuilt side panel that will replace the original kit piece. Use the template provided to trim a pair of new interior side panels from .040 sheet stock (fig. 6-5) The new panels not only provide a smooth surface inside the race car but reflect the stripped-down interior of a '60s stock car. Note that the new side panel is $\frac{1}{16}''$ shorter in height than the stock panel, which will allow the body to sit lower on the chassis. Also, there is a small extender on the aft end of each panel, which provides a solid support for the modified package shelf.

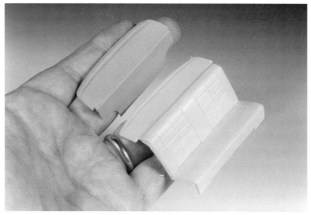

Fig. 6-8. Next, use a razor saw to separate the stock rear seat from the kit package shelf. Use the template provided to make a new rear bulkhead panel (fig. 6-5) and attach it to the kit package shelf as shown here.

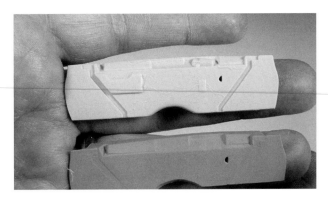

Fig. 6-9. The stock kit firewall is shown here above, compared to the modified unit below. Carefully remove all surface detail, including the heater and molded-in windshield wiper motor. Use body putty to fill in the angled channels where the stock inner front fender panel would be located. You'll have to do more work to the one on the left to make it look like the one on the right. Also, shorten the firewall by 1/16″ in height, as you did on the interior panels.

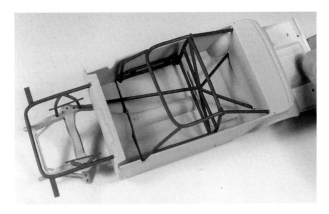

Fig. 6-11. Test-fit the finished roll cage to the interior. Some tweaking may be required here. Check for clearance on either end of the dashboard. Note the addition of a horizontal bar that runs between the front of both roll cage sides across the floor and over the transmission hump.

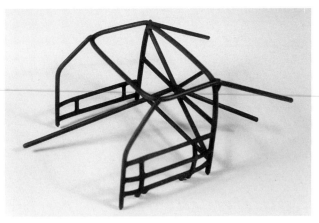

Fig. 6-10. Use fig. 6-6 to construct an accurate roll cage for the half-chassis race car. Start by inserting lengths of .060-diameter brass rod inside 3/32″-diameter plastic tubing. The soft wire will allow you to bend the plastic tubing to shape easily and also allow it to maintain its shape. Here Randy used the roll cage side bars from a Monogram stock car kit to represent this area. He removed two horizontal bars on the right side and one bar on the left to reflect the rules from '66–'67. The front hoop that strengthens the new front subframe uses 3/32″ Evergreen tubing with .060 brass rod inserted inside. Make the structural side uprights that form the shock towers in the same fashion. Then lay a 3/4″ length of .030-diameter rod horizontally to make the actual attachment points for the dual shocks. Finally, add two lengths of .040 sheet plastic to form the "ears," which serve as fender supports and attachment points for the oil cooler and tank.

Figs. 6-12 and 6-13. Next, test-fit the body shell to the chassis with the firewall in place to ensure alignment and proper clearance. Use 1/16″ square bar stock to form the structure that represents the radiator support. Use a small rectangle of .020 sheet stock to form the base plate for the battery tray.

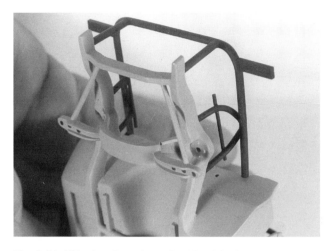

Fig. 6-14. This view from the underside of the front snout shows how the front hoop blends into the front subframe. Note the addition of the lower control arms and struts and the location of the upper coil spring seat, which are all straight from the '65 Galaxie chassis.

Fig. 6-15. In this view the left front spindle with wheel and tire mounted is set in place. Note the lower shock mount made from .060 rod, which attaches across the lower control arm next to the ball joint. Also shown is the steering arm attached to the spindle. Make this piece from .030 brass rod.

Fig. 6-16. Next add scratchbuilt coil springs to the front suspension. Make a pair of coil springs by winding .020 wire. Wrap wire around a piece of tubing.

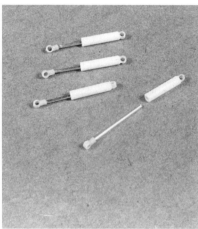

Fig. 6-17. Make eight adjustable shock absorbers like the ones shown here. Use .060-diameter Evergreen rod for the shock absorber body and .030-diameter silver wire for the shaft. Make the upper mounts using short lengths of tubing and the lower mounts from the same materials.

Fig. 6-19. Add short lengths of .060-diameter rod on either side of the rear leaf spring mounting pads. Then attach the shocks to the rod extensions. Add a rear-end cooling pump to the nose of the differential.

Fig. 6-20. Use .020 sheet plastic to make a set of rear spring shackles. Here the shackles are glued to the sides of each rear spring perch. On the full-size race car they were used to adjust ride height. Construct a sheet plastic box that fits around the existing kit fuel tank to form the fuel cell.

Fig. 6-21. Next build a small rectangle from four pieces of 1/16″ plastic bar stock to represent the rear-end cooler. Then cut a matching rectangle from a sheet of Dr. Micro Tool fine-mesh screen to finish the job. With the major modifications completed on the chassis and suspension, perform a final test-fit, including temporarily taping components into place, before painting and detailing.

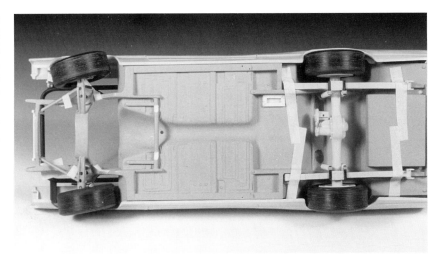

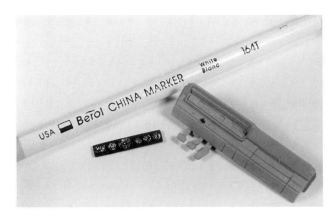

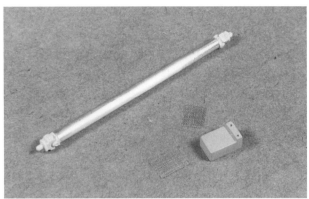

Fig. 6-22. Use the stock Fairlane kit dashboard. Remove the gauge panel from a Monogram stock car kit dash and trim it down to fit into the Fairlane instrument cluster. During final detailing highlight the instrument surface details with white wax marking pencil.

Fig. 6-23. For added detail remove the U joint from the kit drive-shaft. Replace it with a 2¼" length of ³⁄₃₂"-diameter aluminum tubing. Add realism to the engine oil cooler by applying sections of Dr. Micro Tool fine-mesh screen to the front and rear surfaces.

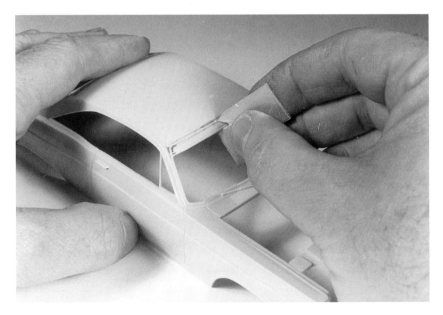

Fig. 6-24. The Ertl/AMT kit body requires the relocation of the front and rear windshield headers. First measure off the area to be modified. Once you have scribed the lines, use an X-Acto knife and jeweler's file to reshape and enlarge the window openings.

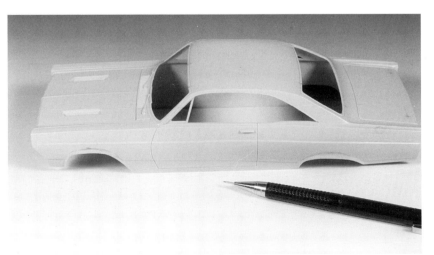

Fig. 6-25. The production body shell requires many small modifications to transform it into a NASCAR stock car. Use a soft lead pencil to sketch the modifications that need to be made before cutting plastic. Fill in the hood depressions, remove the windshield wipers, mark the location for front and rear window retainers, mark the location for hood and deck pins, enlarge the wheel openings, and mark the spot where you'll have to drill a hole for the new fuel filler neck in the left rear fender.

Fig. 6-26. Next, drill a ⅛″-diameter hole in the left rear fender. Then insert a short length of aluminum tubing to represent the filler neck.

Fig. 6-27. File and sand away the molded-in windshield wipers, making sure not to remove too much material from the cowl area. Work carefully to retain the air vent detail in this panel.

Fig. 6-28. You'll have to enlarge the front wheel opening approximately ⅛″ for better tire clearance. First, use an X-Acto knife to cut away enough material in the shape of an arch. Wrap a piece of 320 sandpaper around a common 35mm film canister and true the opening to shape. Randy formed the lip of the new opening by first gluing a strip of 1/16″ bar stock into the opening. When the glue is dry, file and sand the bar stock, inside and outside, to shape. Then use body putty to blend the lip into the exterior surface of the fender. Repeat this process for the rear fender opening and lip. Note here, though, that the arch of the new rear fender opening is much flatter than the one on the front fender.

Fig. 6-29. To add just a touch of additional detail, carefully remove the molded-in material from inside each door handle. Use a .020″-diameter drill bit to methodically drill out this area. Then use an X-Acto knife and small file to clean up the door surfaces.

Final comments

To complete the '66–'67 Fairlane half-chassis car, remember that the interior of most Holman-Moody race cars were finished off with flat black on the dash top, upper door panels, and package shelf. The interior floor should be painted Testor's Gull Gray.

Finish the front of the dash, interior side panels, and rear bulkhead in aluminum. Paint the roll cage assembly flat black and add vinyl tubing to represent the padding. Finish the chassis in Testor's Gull Gray, highlighting the suspension and driveline parts with shades of metallic and black paints for contrast.

Testor's offers many paint colors that closely resemble the actual race car finishes, and companies like BSR, MCW, and Tru-Match produce authentic race car paint colors.

Slixx, Fred Cady, Blue Ridge, and JNJ have produced water-slide decals for many of these finished models.

MIGHTY MOPARS

BUILDING A 1967 PLYMOUTH GTX AND DETAILING A PLYMOUTH SUPERBIRD

This Brad Knight 1967 Petty Plymouth was converted from a Revell plastic kit by using lots of good reference materials, kitbashing parts from other kits, and hand-making whatever else was needed. Jim Kampman photo.

This model of the 1970 Petty Superbird was built from the original Jo-Han kit. The body shell was kitbashed with an interior from an AMT Chevelle stock car, a modified short track MPC Firebird kit, suspension parts from a 1970 MPC Charger, and front suspension and snout pieces from an early '70s MPC stock car. The paint is Plymouth Basin Street Blue (Petty Blue) acrylic enamel. The decals are from various Cady Design, JNJ, and Slixx sheets.

With the start of the 1967 NASCAR Grand National season, the sport had survived its greatest challenge to date. The death-grip battle for control between Chrysler and Ford appeared to be at an end. Bill France Sr. had laid down the rules for the new season in late 1966, and that leveled the playing field just about as much as was humanly possible. Ford was back for '67 with their wedge 427-powered Fairlanes and Mercury Comets, which received begrudging approval from the sanctioning body late in the 1966 season. Ford Motor Company had for the most part given up the idea of ever using their overhead cam 427 in NASCAR competition.

On the other side, Chrysler had wrestled approval from NASCAR for the continued use of their potent Hemi engine. The rules required the big V-8 be limited to 404 cid on the super speedways and only used at a full-bore 426 cid on the short tracks.

As the 1967 season unfolded, no one had a clue to the significant accomplishments that lay ahead. For Richard Petty 1967 would mark his second of seven championships, but that was not all. Of the 48 events contested on the schedule, Petty won a whopping 27 races, finished in the top five 38 times, and recorded 40 finishes in the top ten—and he completed 41 of the 48 races. And this was not the best part of the story!

It all started with a win at the short track in Winston-Salem, North Carolina, in mid-August. Then Petty won the next race and the next. By October 1, Richard Petty had won an incredible ten straight races! This remains an all-time record for any driver in NASCAR history. The car that Petty drove to most of those ten-straight victories now resides in the Joe Weatherly Museum at Darlington International Speedway, South Carolina.

The technology used in constructing Dodge and Plymouth race cars remained fairly consistent from 1966 through 1970. Suspension, drive train, chassis, interiors, and so on, were nearly identical for the '66–'67 Plymouth Satellite and GTX, '66–'67 Dodge Charger, 1968–70 Plymouth Road Runner, 1968, '69, and '70 Dodge Charger, 1969 Charger 500 and Daytona, and the 1970 Plymouth Superbird. All these models, whether street-driven or race car, started life on a factory unibody platform with front and rear subframes.

With this knowledge, building scale replicas of any of the Dodges and Plymouths of this era is made a lot easier for the stock car modeler. Follow along with us now as Brad Knight and I describe how to build the Petty 1967 Plymouth. Some of the items you'll need for this project include:
• Revell 1967 Plymouth GTX 1/25 scale kit
• Monogram NASCAR Thunderbird kit
• various diameters of plastic rod and tubing
• various thicknesses of sheet plastic
• Tru-Match Petty Blue, "the early years" spray paint
• Slixx decal sheet no. 1019/6743
• resin stock car wheels, accessory items like oil reservoirs, oil coolers, and cooling fan shrouds

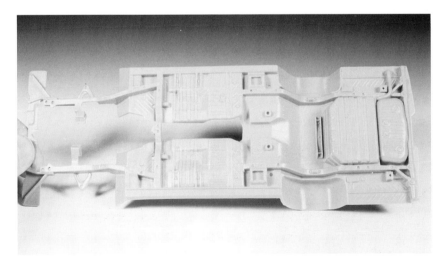

Fig. 7-3. Start by removing the molded-in gas tank and trunk floor from the rear of the '67 kit chassis. Also grind away the gas filler neck and the mounting points for the stock dual exhaust pipes. Make a new chassis floor using .020 sheet plastic to fill in this area between the subframe rails. Jim Kampman photo.

Fig. 7-4. Brad decided to lift the interior from an Ertl/AMT Matador race car kit, since it already had many of the stripped-down modifications. Jim Kampman photo.

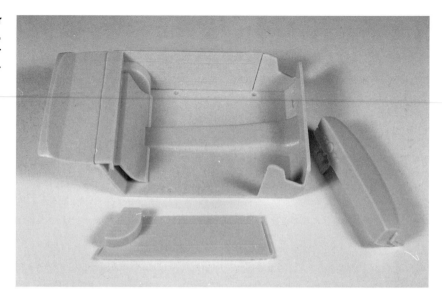

Fig. 7-5. Shown here are the four main structural components of Brad Knight's '67 Petty Plymouth. In the foreground are the roll cage and modified Matador interior, ready for primer and paint. In the center is the Revell GTX chassis with the new fuel cell in place between the rear subframe rails, and the modified front hoop from a Monogram T-Bird kit attached to the front subframe rails and the firewall. In the background is the '67 race car body shell modified from the stock Revell kit. All trim, emblems, and script and front inner fender panels have been removed. Jim Kampman photo.

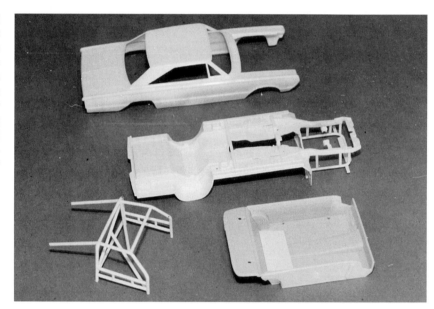

Fig. 7-6. Note the size and shape of the revised rear wheel opening. Take some extra time occasionally to test-fit all parts and assemblies. This is particularly true for semi-scratch projects like this Brad knight '67 Petty Plymouth. Brad built the '70 Petty Plymouth from the original Jo-Han Superbird 1/25 scale kit. It required extensive modifications, as this kit is primarily molded as a street-driven vehicle. Note the radius of the front wheel opening and the enlargement of the rear wheel opening. Both procedures are executed for race car tire clearance and to allow a lower ride. Jim Kampman photo.

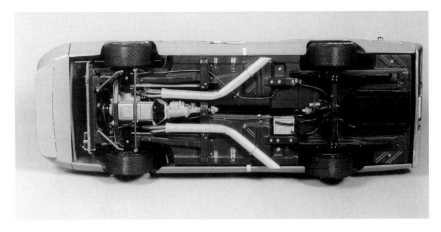

Figs. 7-7 and 7-8. These chassis views of the '70 Petty Superbird show that the underside demands as much attention as any other part of a race car model. Note the rear-end plumbing, oil cooler and pump, brake and fuel lines, and exhaust dumps hand-formed from 3/32" aluminum tubing. This close-up view of the Superbird shows the solid rear axle mounted on leaf springs featuring an axle stiffener, oil cooler and pump. You'll have to completely grind away the molded-in rear suspension on the Jo-Han kit chassis and box in the area with .020 sheet plastic. The new axle and rear springs came from a '69 MPC Charger kit.

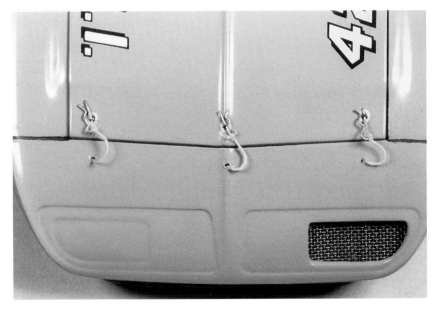

Fig. 7-9. Hood pins of some sort are a necessity on a well-detailed stock car model. Make them from thin steel wire, sewing needles, and silver thread. Paint on the scuff plates under each retainer clip with silver bottle paint and a small brush.

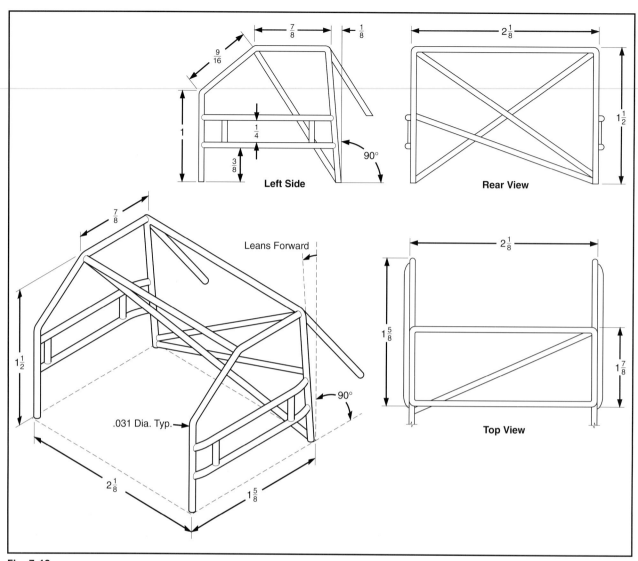

Left Side

Rear View

Leans Forward

90°

.031 Dia. Typ.

90°

Top View

Fig. 7-10

Fig. 7-11. Adding wheel weights and valve stems can greatly enhance wheel and tire detail. The wheel weights are actually a dab of white glue painted aluminum. The valve stem is a short length of wire painted black with a silver cap. Note the paint detail on the grease cap over the end of the front spindle and the five lug nuts. You can do the lettering on the tires with a steady hand, a 5-0 brush, and Sign Painters One-Shot White.

DETAILING A SUPERBIRD

The chassis

The major modification to the Revell GTX kit chassis is replacing the production gas tank with a fuel cell. Cut away the entire area between the rear subframe rails, including the stock gas tank and trunk floor well. Replace the chassis floor with .020 sheet plastic cut to fit in the new opening. Next, construct a fuel cell from .030 sheet plastic.

The front and rear kit suspension is fairly accurate for use under a race car. Add a pair of shock absorbers to either end of the rear axle. The lower components of the kit front suspension will also work well for this application.

Then install the firewall in place on the chassis. Next, insert the chassis into the body shell. Test-fit the front hoop from the Monogram T-Bird kit to the top front of the subframe of the kit chassis and against the firewall. Attach the hoop to the firewall and adjust the length of the six vertical posts to keep it level with the front frame rails. Assemble the kit front suspension and provide for shock mounts to the horizontal hoop bars for the dual front shock absorbers.

The power plant

The Revell kit Hemi engine is quite adequate for use in this race car model. Add a racing air cleaner over the single four-barrel carb. Replace the cast-iron exhaust headers with tubular-type headers. Next, add oil breathers to both valve covers along with a filler neck to the front of the right valve cover. Most Hemi racing engines built by Maurice Petty had a quick-fill tube running between the valve covers as shown here. Make this piece from a length of $1/16''$ plastic rod. Add a pair of oil breathers side by side in the center of the tube.

Mount the ignition coil to the front of the right valve cover. Attach the engine oil cooler to the driver's side of the front hoop bars next to the radiator. Add the oil cooler to the passenger's side of the radiator in the engine compartment. Both cooler and reservoir are resin pieces from the Modelhaus.

The interior

Brad Knight used the interior tub from the Ertl/AMT NASCAR Matador kit. If you decide to go this route, assemble the Matador interior according to the kit instructions. Once placed in position on top of the Plymouth chassis, the rear floor of the Matador interior will require some trial-and-error modification to clear the platform riser so the floor of the interior sits parallel with the chassis.

Roll cages used in Petty race cars of this period were of an unusual configuration. Build the roll cage for this 1967 Petty Plymouth using $5/32''$ plastic rod, working from the measurements and diagram provided (fig. 7-10).

Wheels and tires

The best choice for racing wheels for this Plymouth is the Holman-Moody–style resin items available from the Modelhaus. The proper choice of rubber for a 1967 through 1970 NASCAR Grand national race car is the treaded tires that originally came in the MPC Grand National and later Southern Stocker series. These tires were available most recently in reissues of AMT '70s stock cars. These tires have a $7/16''$ tread width and are imprinted on the sidewall with the designation "8.50 - 12.00 x 15."

The body shell

Start by removing all body emblems and trim including fender ornaments and cut away the inner fender panels molded to the inside of the front fenders with a razor saw. You'll have to remove the rocker panel trim along with the front wheel lip moldings. Complete the body shell modifications by enlarging the rear wheel openings as shown in the accompanying photos. Remember to install the exterior door handles during final assembly.

Painting

Follow this detailed listing of specific parts of the model and the color that each one should be painted:
- Body shell, hood, firewall, front hoop and chassis, interior surfaces, and roll cage:

  Tru-Match Petty Blue, "the early years"
- wheels: dark blue
- gas cap: fluorescent red
- interior door panels: aluminum
- driver's seat and bolster: flat black
- dash top: flat black
- instrument panel: aluminum
- radiator: aluminum
- air cleaner: gloss black
- valve covers: semigloss black
- engine block: steel
- headers: gunmetal
- hood hinges: gloss black

Once the exterior body finish is thoroughly dry, rub out the final coat of paint with an LMG polishing kit. You may only need to use the 8000- and 12000-grit cloth to bring the smoothness of the paint surface around. Top this off with a generous round of the Micro Gloss polish contained in the kit. Remember, never wax the paint finish before applying decals.

Final assembly can include engine detailing like the electrical wiring and oil cooling lines connecting the engine, reservoir, and cooler. Chassis details can include brake fluid lines, along with plumbing for the rear-end cooler. The building and detailing techniques presented here can be used to build a variety of Dodges and Plymouths from 1966 through 1970.

SANGUINE '70s

BUILDING AND DETAILING THREE NASCAR RACE CARS FROM THE 1970S

This shelf model of the Petty Enterprises' Dodge driven by Buddy Baker in 1971 was built by Drew Hierwarter. The kit is an original MPC NASCAR Charger kit of the car built right from the box.

The Bud Moore no. 15 Ford Torino driven by David Pearson in early 1972. Equipped with a 351 cid small-block V-8 engine and competing against big-black juggernauts, this was the first successful NASCAR race car with a small-displacement engine. This model was built from an All-American Models resin body and Gofer racing interior and chassis kits.

NASCAR racing in the decade of the '70s opened on a low note. The special-bodied race cars like the Charger Daytona, Plymouth Superbird, Ford Talledega, and Mercury Cyclone were handicapped so severely that NASCAR might as well have just banned them outright. The last appearance of a winged car was the Golden Products Daytona in the 1971 500. Limited to a minuscule 5-liter (305 cid) engine, Dick Brooks was able to stay competitive with the 7-liter (426-7 cid) powered race cars during the race until rumpled body work ruined the car's aerodynamics.

Ford Motor Company withdrew their support partway through the 1971 season, effectively putting Holman-Moody out of the factory-backed stock car racing business. For the '71 season Chrysler cut back their factory involvement, providing support only for a Plymouth and a Dodge fielded by Petty Enterprises. But while Ford and Chrysler were beating a hasty retreat to the exits, General Motors and American Motors were making their presence known.

On the up side, Chevrolet returned to the series in 1971 backing a Monte Carlo built by the legendary Junior Johnson and driven by midwesterner Charlie Glotzbach. AMC approached racing mogul Roger Penske about fielding a Matador in the high-profile stock car series. Holman-Moody built a pair of '72 "Bullfighters" for Penske, and the late racing legend Mark Donahue won the marque's first race in 1973.

The Arab oil crises of 1973 and 1979 took a heavy toll on the American auto industry. And that in turn had an unsettling ripple effect throughout motorsport and in particular on NASCAR. Some car makers were forced to drastically downsize their products, while others were just struggling to stay alive. NASCAR was slow to make drastic changes to the size and shape of their cars. During the late '70s

Dodge, Plymouth, and Mercury disappeared permanently from competition. Approval of the 350 cid Chevrolet V-8 engine for use in other intermediate GM race cars brought factory backing from Buick and Pontiac to join Oldsmobile and Chevrolet, who were already in the thick of the hunt.

The best news for NASCAR stock car racing in the 1970s was securing a high-dollar series sponsor. RJR-Nabisco stepped up and propelled NASCAR racing rapidly forward by sponsoring the "Winston Cup series," today a common household term. Television coverage also became commonplace during the '70s. The 1979 Daytona 500 was telecast live by CBS for the first time. Quickly NASCAR racing gained repectability and millions of fans worldwide.

For the stock car modeler the '70s got off to a rousing start. MPC, AMT, and Jo-Han introduced 1/25 scale race car models to a hungry modeling public. The many kits produced then (P37, P38, P39) included a Petty Plymouth and three Dodge Chargers, a Charger Daytona, two different Ford Torinos, a Mercury Montego, four different Chevrolet Chevelles, two different Monte Carlos, a Pontiac GTO (with a clear see-through body shell, no less), and an AMC Matador. The last of this series was an MPC 1976 Chevrolet Laguna.

When Detroit downsized and NASCAR didn't, stock car teams turned to the 1977 Oldsmobile Cutlass S with an angled nose much like that of the Chevy Laguna and the 1977 Monte Carlo. These two body styles were used almost exclusively through the 1980 season by GM teams. The model kit manufacturers did not follow the NASCAR lead. What followed was a drought for the race car modelers that lasted until 1983.

Three project cars

Let's take a look at building and detailing three stock car models that represent not only NASCAR race cars

of the '70s but three different building approaches.

1972 Ford Torino

The no. 15 Bud Moore Torino shown here represents a pivotal point in NASCAR history. Fresh from building Trans-Am Mustangs for Parnelli Jones, Moore brought what he had learned in that series into stock car racing in 1972. The Moore '72 Torino was the very first successful small-block NASCAR stocker. At a time when the competition still sported nearly a 100 cid advantage, Bud Moore stuck with his Trans-Am proven small-block 351 cid V-8. It was David versus three dozen Goliaths. This race car, driven at times by David Pearson, George Fulmer, Darrell Waltrip, Bobby Issac, and Buddy Baker, changed NASCAR engine technology forever.

What you will need for this project:
• Jo-Han kit no. C-3372 '72 Torino or
• All American Models 1972 Torino resin body shell and
• Gofer Racing Historic Roll Cage and Interior
• Gofer Racing Historic Stock Racing Chassis
• Gofer Racing Historic Wheels and Tires
• Jo-Han snap kit no. CS-502 (correct hood donor)
• Ertl/AMT late model Ford stock car (engine donor)
• Model Car World paint: Ford Grabber Orange
• Dave Romero decals: no. 15 Bud Moore Ford or
• Fred Cady Design: no. 15 Sta-Powr Torino, no. 15 RC Cola Torino

This historic NASCAR stock car model is built using the All-American Models resin body, the Gofer interior and chassis parts, Dave Romero decals, MCW Grabber Orange acrylic lacquer, Modelhaus resin wheels, the small-block Ford engine from Ertl/AMT, and tires from the Ertl/AMT Coca-Cola Matador kit.

Fig. 8-3. If you're using the kit styrene body shell, first remove all trim, scripts, nameplates, and badging. Whether you're using the kit or resin body, you'll have to raise the arch of the wheel openings in the front fenders to provide added clearance for the fat racing tires. This modification will also allow you to lower the front of the car for a more aggressive stance. First mark the cut to make. Take out about ⅛˝ of material. Once the excess material is cut away, slide the wheel opening arch up and glue it into position. Use micro-balloons and super glue as a filler or a small amount of body putty to clean up the modifications.

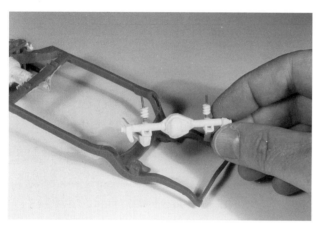

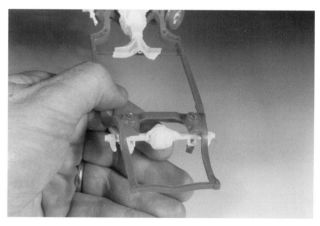

Fig. 8-4. Tack the rear axle and trailing arms together on the instruction sheet. Next, drill a hole straight through both rear coil springs. Cut two ½˝ lengths of .030 plastic rod and run them through each spring. Leave about ⅛˝ sticking out at the bottom. Finally, drill a starter hole where each spring attaches to the axle housing and glue the modified coils in place.

Fig. 8-5. Then drill two holes where the top of each coil spring attaches to the spring tower in the frame. Insert each plastic rod protruding from the coils through these holes. This will allow you to adjust the rear suspension height during final assembly.

Fig. 8-6. Assemble the Gofer chassis, front suspension, and snout. Glue the basic pieces of the Ertl/AMT small-block racing engine together. Temporarily tape the engine into place in the engine bay. This allows you to determine whether the transmission tail shaft has to be shortened, whether the driveshaft is too long or short, whether the oil pump at the lower right front corner of the engine clears the frame and suspension, and whether there is sufficient clearance between the cylinder heads and top control arms to route the exhaust headers.

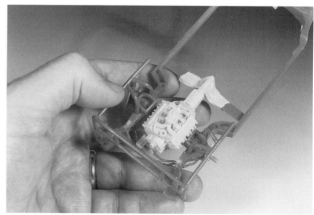

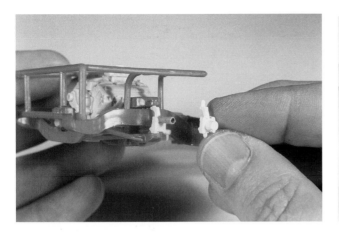

Figs. 8-7 and 8-8. Since you have raised the wheel arch opening in both front fenders, you'll have to lower the ride height to eliminate the excessive clearance above the front tires and the fender opening. First remove the axle protruding from each front spindle. Drill a .070″ hole farther up the face of each spindle. Cut a ⅜″ length of .060 plastic rod or tubing and glue into place in the new hole in each spindle. This will allow the nose of the race car to be adjusted downward.

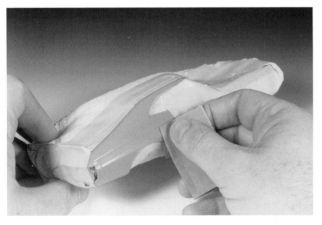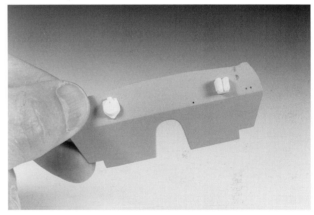

Fig. 8-9. Once the body work is complete, glue the major pieces of the roll cage and interior together, allowing the dashboard, rear bulkhead, and cage to be separated for painting. Plastic-kote T-235 automotive primer is an essential barrier coat if you are working with a styrene body shell. I use this primer on everything regardless of what final paint I'm using. Here the body gets generous coats of MCW Ford Grabber Orange. Paint all the interior parts with Tru-Match Roll Cage Gray. Whenever paint masking is required, use 3M ⅛″ blue pinstriping tape along the primary edge. Then use ½″ masking tape attached to a sheet of paper towel and overlap the outside edge of the striping tape. You may discover a flaw in the final paint finish on your model. Rather than respraying the whole body, mask off just the affected area along major body lines and panel seams. Sand it smooth, then wipe the area down with rubbing alcohol and repaint that portion of the model.

Fig. 8-10. The Gofer kit firewall is totally devoid of surface detail. Carefully remove the surge tank and dual brake master cylinder from a Monogram stock car kit. Then transplant the two pieces onto the Gofer firewall.

Fig. 8-11. Occasional test-fitting during construction is time well spent. Temporarily assemble the body, chassis, engine, and front wheels and tires. Now you can see the actual location of components that will be linked together during final detailing. This will help you decide what holes need to be drilled where and the best route for fuel, brake, and oil cooling lines, as well as the location of the top and bottom radiator hoses. Test-fitting also allows you to determine the route and location of rear-end plumbing, brake lines, and the positioning of the exhaust pipe dumps.

Fig. 8-12. As part of the final detailing of the Torino interior, add Scale Model Speedways roll bar padding, seat belts to the driver's seat, and gauge face details with a brush and bottle paints to the dashboard instruments. The battery and fuel cell can be optional on this model, since the trunk lid does not open and both are not visible when the model is finished.

Fig. 8-13. The Gofer Historic Stock Car chassis and interior are molded as individual components. This is a handy feature, allowing each to be worked on separately.

Fig. 8-14. You'll have to assemble some of the engine plumbing before gluing it into the chassis. Here the plug and coil wire are in place, along with the primary oil cooling lines replicated with silver craft braid. Bend lengths of .090 solid-core solder into shape to represent the top and bottom radiator hoses. Drill a small hole and insert a short length of wire in the ends of the solder. Then drill corresponding holes in the radiator, which will aid in holding the hoses in place.

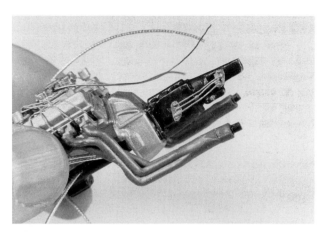

Fig. 8-15. Construct a realistic-looking shifting linkage mechanism for the transmission using two small pieces of .010 sheet plastic for the brackets. Use uncoated steel wire for the shift linkages.

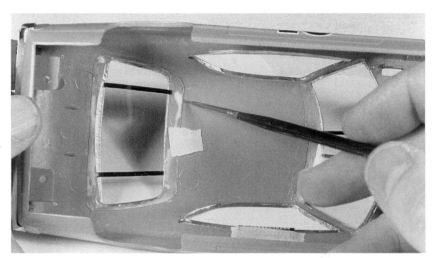

Fig. 8-16. Use Sobo white craft glue to hold the front and rear windows in place. For best results, use a 3-0 brush and dab on a small amount of white glue around the edges of the window opening. Carefully insert the glass into place and use masking tape to hold it until dry. Wipe away any excess glue with a damp cloth.

Fig. 8-17. The type of driver safety window net used in the '70s was more like screening than the heavy webbing used today. This window net is made from a section of vinyl screen taken from an auto body repair kit. Apply 1/16″ strips of masking tape around the edges and paint flat black. Attach the screen inside the window opening between the body and roll cage bars. Drape the screen out the window and tack it in place with a minute drop of white craft glue.

1972 Petty/STP Plymouth

Short of starting with a very old and very expensive race car model kit, sometimes you may have no choice but to modify a current street-stock plastic kit. Many of the tips and techniques that we have already covered in earlier chapters can easily be applied on this project. Though by the '70s some of the technology had evolved a bit further, surprisingly the chassis, suspension, and driveline of the average stock car had changed only slightly.

Brad Knight tackled the building of this Petty/STP Plymouth model in a very thorough and straightforward fashion. This replica is built the old-fashioned way—using good reference material, patience, and excellent scratchbuilding techniques.

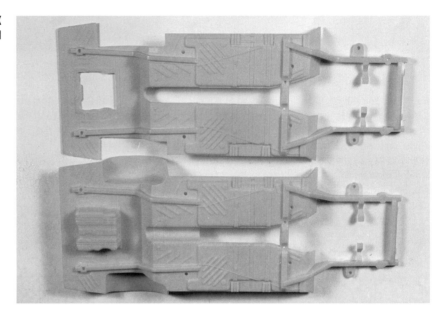

Fig. 8-18. Starting with the Revell '71 GTX kit chassis, remove the existing stock fuel tank and the driveshaft tunnel.

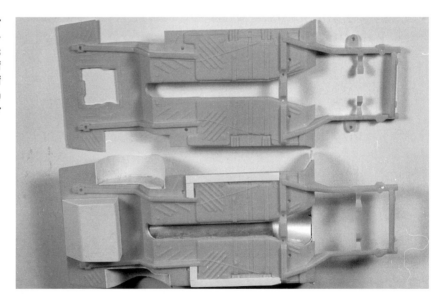

Fig. 8-19. Next, remove the stock rear inner fender panels and enlarge the opening in the chassis sides to the dimensions shown in fig. 8-23. Box in the perimeter of the kit frame using 1/16″ x 5/32″ strips of sheet plastic. This modification serves to tie the front and rear subframes together into one unit.

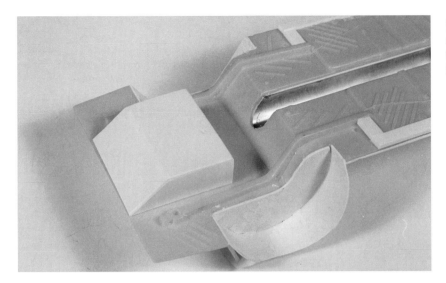

Fig. 8-20. Using .020 sheet plastic, build a fuel cell measuring 1.25″ long by 1.3″ wide by .40″ in height. Fabricate a pair of floor panels from .020 plastic.

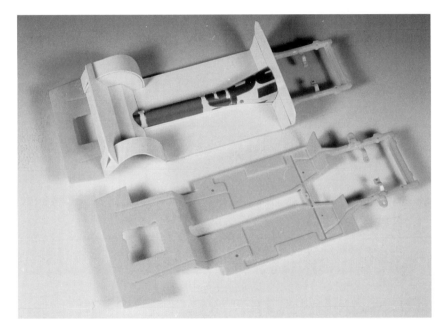

Figs. 8-21 and 8-22. Fabricate new rear wheel wells by cutting out two 1.5″-diameter circles from .020 sheet plastic. Glue them to the frame so they are located ½″ above the surface of the interior floor. Next, make the remaining part of the panel from .020 sheet plastic from the shape shown in fig. 8-25. Then bend these panels around the perimeter of the circles and glue into place. Some sanding may be required to modify this assembly to fit the inside curvature of the Plymouth body shell. Then fabricate a new firewall and a new rear bulkhead from .040 sheet plastic, using the templates in fig 8-26. Next, make a new driveshaft tunnel from thin sheet aluminum rolled gently around the handle of an X-Acto knife, shaped into an arc to fit the opening in the kit chassis. Brad uses this material from the sides of a 12-ounce soda can. The driveshaft tunnel is approximately ⅞″ in width by 2⅞″ in length. Now, cut out a new transmission hump from the thin sheet aluminum, using the basic shape shown in fig. 8-27. Again, gently roll the aluminum around the knife handle to achieve the proper arc to fit the opening in the kit chassis.

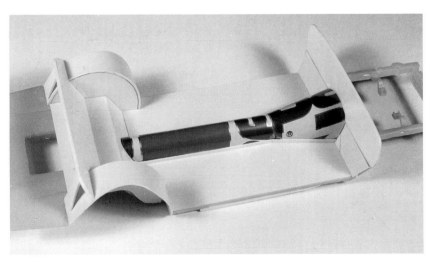

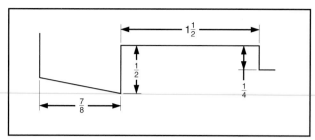

Fig. 8-23

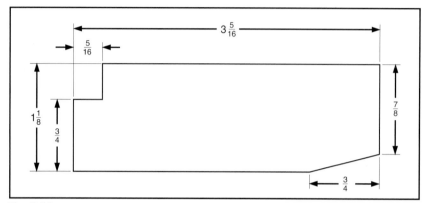

Fig. 8-24

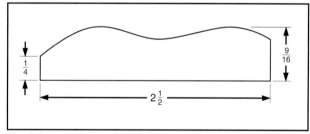

Fig. 8-25

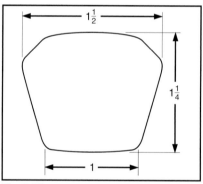

Fig. 8-27

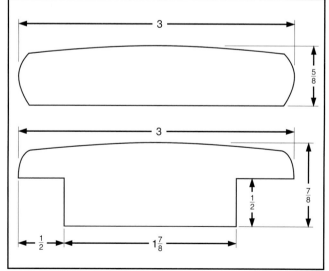

Fig. 8-26

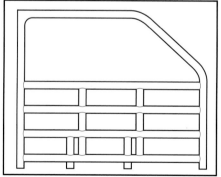

Fig. 8-28

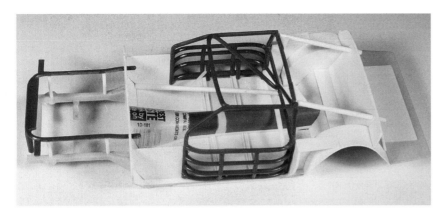

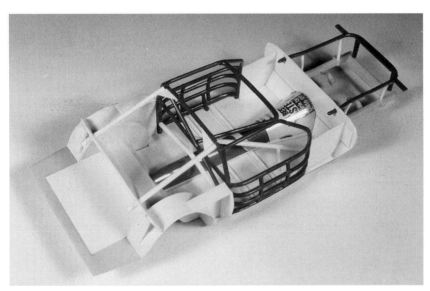

Figs. 8-29 and 8-30. Then alter the roll cage from a Monogram NASCAR Thunderbird kit by removing the front and rear crush panels. Next, remove the lower portion of the vertical bars so that only short pieces of the horizontal bars remain as shown in fig. 8-28. Position the assembled roll cage approximately ⅞″ from the fire wall. Construct new side crush panels from .020 sheet plastic at all four corners of the roll cage. Next, using the front hoop from the Monogram T-Bird kit, cut away all vertical bars except for the two in front. Once the modified hoop is mounted between the firewall and frame, measure the distance between the hoop bars and the frame rails. Cut four lengths of .060 plastic rod and glue into place between the hoop and frame.

Fig. 8-31. Remove the front inner fender panels from the GTX kit body shell. Be careful to retain the small lip along the sides of the opening between fenders to help keep the hood in place.

Fig. 8-32. Also remove the rocker panel trim and front and rear wheel opening molding. Fill in the side marker lights with body filler. Glue the movable air grabber hood scoop in place. Sand and fill to blend in the seam.

Figs. 8-33 and 8-34. Take a moment to test-fit the chassis and roll cage into the body shell to make sure everything lines up before proceeding.

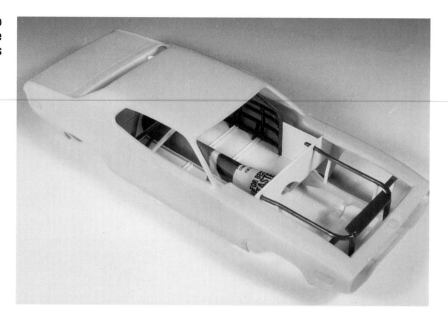

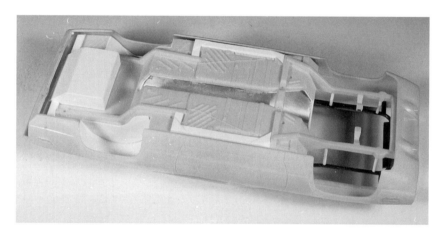

Fig. 8-35. Once the preceding steps have been competed, the chassis, interior, and body shell are ready for the next step of priming and painting.

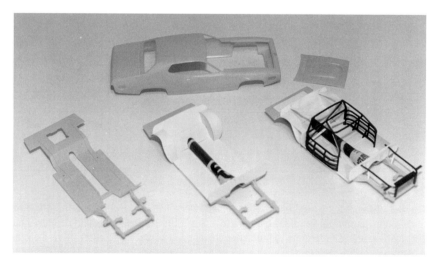

Conclusion

From this point on, the '71 Plymouth goes together much like most Chevrolet, Ford, Dodge, and Mercury NASCAR race cars of the era. Add dual shocks front and rear to the kit suspension pieces. As for a power plant, Brad Knight used the Hemi engine from Monogram's 1971 'Cuda kit, which is precisely what propelled this Petty-built Plymouth. The addition of headers, oil cooling accessories, electrical wiring, fuel lines and air-craft-type fluid lines completes the engine compartment and chassis detailing.

Paint for this vintage model is BSR Replicas and Finshes' Petty Blue and STP Red acrylic enamels. Of course, the chassis, interior, and roll cage all get painted Petty Blue. The decals are from Slixx, sheet no. 1080/7243. Use the Goodyear racing tires from any of the early Monogram stock car kits as well as the five-slot wheels like those found in any of the early Banjo Matthews's rear-steer chassised Monogram T-Bird kit.

1977 Chevrolet Monte Carlo

After the '76 season, NASCAR virtually banned the highly successful Chevrolet Laguna S3 by mandating a limit to 5 liters under the hood. One of the alternate body shells the GM teams turned to was the '77 Chevrolet Monte Carlo. Though admittedly not the most aerodynamic shape at high speed, the MC proved to be a hit on virtually any racing surface it saw competition.

Suprisingly, no styrene 1/25–24 scale model, either street-stock or race car, has ever been produced of this legendary car. Like many of the famous racing stock car body styles, the choice is a completely scratchbuilt body shell or resin. Model Car World offers a resin '77 MC designed specifically to fit a stretched Monogram kit chassis. JNJ Hobbies has also produced a resin '77 Monte Carlo body shell, but this one is decidedly 1/25 scale. The body shell proportions are a bit different from those of the MCW resin body, but with the right paint and decals this model can be built into a respectable replica.

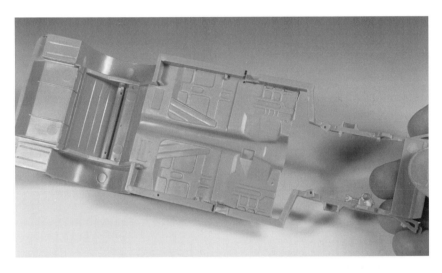

Fig. 8-36. Using two Monogram stock car kit chassis, first mark both of them to be cut. Measure from the front of the frame at the leading edge of the floor back 1¼″ on chassis number 1. Repeat the process on chassis number 2, only this time measure back along the outside frame rail 1¹⁄₁₆″. Cut through both outside frame rails on both chassis. Then cut along each side so as to separate the front subframe from the platform floor. Reassemble the long frame pieces to produce a chassis with a scale 115-inch wheelbase. Make sure all parts are aligned squarely. Use a solid flat surface when realigning and gluing these pieces back together.

Fig. 8-37. Simply drop one of the many resin bodies available of race cars from the mid-to-late '70s down over the length-ened chassis to ensure that the wheels match the fender openings. Shown here on the top is the kit chassis straight from the Monogram kit box. On the bottom is the stretched version required for the 115-inch wheelbase cars.

Fig. 8-38. The front hoop, transmission brace, and driveshaft will also need modifications. Marked here in black are the three parts and the area that requires lengthening.

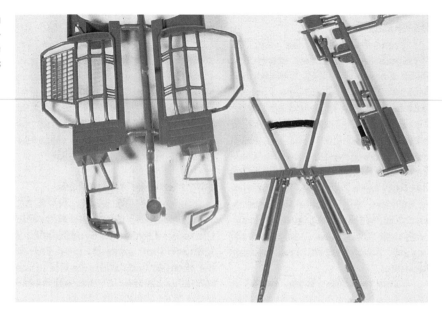

Fig. 8-39. Dave Dodge built this replica of Dale Earnhardt's rookie '77 Monte Carlo. The body shell is resin from MCW, and the two-tone paint is from the same company. The chassis is a modified Monogram stock car unit stretched from 110 to 115 scale inches. The decals are aftermarket items from JNJ.

Fig. 8-40. An MCW '77 Monte Carlo resin body shell designed for the stretched Monogram chassis. Once the minor adjustments are made for the roll cage, hoop, and driveshaft, the model builds up just like any styrene glue kit. Paint for the '77 MCs driven by Dale Earnhardt, Richard Petty, and Darrell Waltrip is available from Model Car World. Water-slide decals for these models are available from BSR Replicas and Finishes.

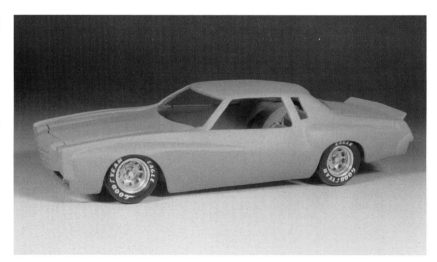

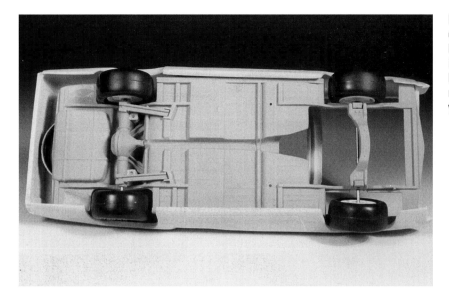

Fig. 8-41. JNJ Hobbies at one time produced a resin '77 Monte Carlo body shell, but this one is decidedly 1/25 scale. This is the JNJ MC riding on an AMT/Ertl Matador styrene kit chassis. This body is no longer on the market. If you're lucky, you may run across one somewhere.

MPC stock car kits

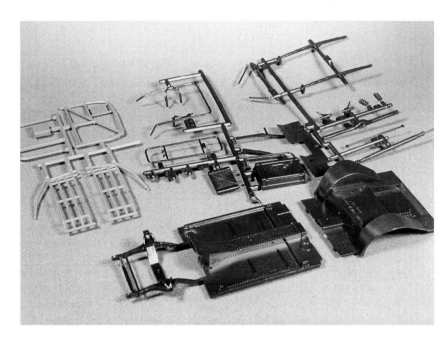

Fig. 8-42. The novel MPC adjustable chassis allowed it to be used under a variety of body shells. However, the chassis was not quite correct for the Ford and GM cars and was totally incorrect for the Dodges and Plymouths.

Fig. 8-43. Using pieces of plastic sheet and bar stock to correct the frame and chassis plate and adding the rear axle and suspension from a Monogram stock car kit brings the MPC chassis up to standards.

9

THE GOLDEN ERA

BUILDING AND DETAILING THE FIRST MONOGRAM GM NASCAR KITS

The Miller Buick that Bobby Allison drove to the 1983 Winston Cup championship. The body color is Plasti-kote bright white gloss acrylic enamel applied over Plasti-kote T-235 light gray sandable primer. This type of primer is absolutely essential to provide a barrier coat so that the "hotter" automotive finishes do not attack the surface of the polystyrene plastic.

Prior to the 1981 Grand National season, NASCAR finally instituted new rules governing the sport and, in particular, the construction of race cars for the series. The automobile manufacturers began industry-wide downsizing with the 1977 model year and by 1980 most General Motors street-driven cars were quite a bit smaller. Freshly restyled for 1981 was the popular quartet of Chevrolet Monte Carlo, Pontiac Grand Prix, Buick Regal, and Oldsmobile Cutlass. The rule book called for a reduction of overall length and set the new wheelbase requirements for all manufacturers' race cars at 110 inches, down from the long-standing dimension of 115 inches.

Unaffected by the new rules was the track width of the race car, the dis-

tance measured center to center of the front wheels. To reduce that dimension would have required either narrowing the chassis (a prohibitive expense) or a new and much narrower racing tire from Goodyear. Instead, NASCAR decided to maintain the previous width of the race cars, which necessitated allowing hand-formed body panels that puckered the side sheet metal around the wheel openings to keep the tires inside the body. Now even less of a race car's sheet metal originated in Detroit.

For the first time since the mid-'70s, a model manufacturer took notice of the ever-growing popularity of stock car racing and the continual clamoring of the model-car-building community for something brand new to build. Monogram Models in 1983,

as part of a four-car series, introduced two new NASCAR stock car kits. The first of the two releases were 1/24 models of Buick Regals riding on a highly detailed Hutcherson-Pagan "front steer" chassis. The level of detail and authenticity was something never seen previously in this type of model kit.

Other versions of the '83 Regal were followed closely by a Monte Carlo SS and a Pontiac Grand Prix. The availability of these benchmark kits spawned a new industry of aftermarket accessories. Quickly these cottage industries responded with detailing items and a whole new market was created for stock car decals. Fred Cady Design, JNJ Hobbies, Blue Ridge, DNL, BSR, Chimneyville, and Slixx—just to mention a few—produced accurate water-slide markings for just about any of the NASCAR stock cars that were competing on the nation's speedways.

Ultimately, that original Monogram Hutcherson-Pagan front-steer chassis was the underpinning for several NASCAR stock cars kits, including the following:

Chevrolet
1983–85 Monte Carlo "notchback"
1986–87 Monte Carlo SS aero-coupe, "bubbleback"
Buick
1981–85 Regal
1988–91 Regal

Oldsmobile
1987 Delta 88
1988–92 Cutlass
Pontiac
1981–85 Grand Prix
1988–95 Grand Prix

These Monogram stock car are only part of the single most successful model kit series in history. Currently, the total kit sales number in the millions of units, and the series helped launch hundreds of aftermarket parts, pieces, detailing items, and of course literally dozen and dozens of stock car decal sheets.

And when Monogram was not able to produce a particular version of a race car, the aftermarket quickly responded again with conversion kits or complete body shells in resin. Included on this list would be both a conversion kit and resin body for the 1986–87 Buick LeSabre from JNJ Hobbies, All-American Models resin body shell for the 1986–87 Pontiac 2+2, and the 1981–83 Pontiac LeMans resin body shell from Model Car World.

Follow along now as we look at building and detailing tips and techniques that will turn your next stock car project into a contest challenger.

Engine detailing

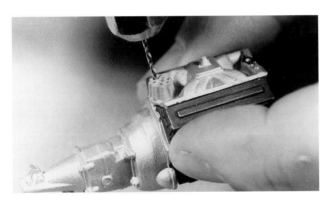

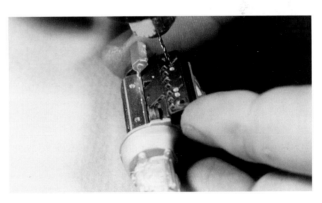

Fig. 9-2. After assembling the basic engine parts, filling the seams, and sanding, prime all parts and apply the following Testor's bottle paint colors: engine block and exhaust headers, steel; cylinder heads, gunmetal; and the intake manifold and transmission, aluminum. Then, carefully drill eight .020″ holes where each spark plug wire is inserted into the top of the distributor cap.

Fig. 9-3. Next drill corresponding holes for each of the eight spark plugs. For this small-displacement GM V-8, the plugs are grouped in four sets of two, positioned side by side between the exhaust ports on the outside surface of each cylinder head.

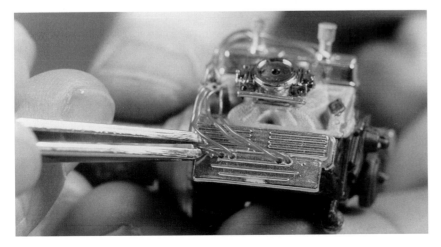

Fig. 9-4. Provide enough slack in each wire to allow for a natural drape over the engine surfaces.

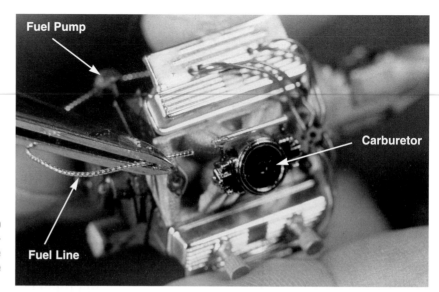

Fuel Pump

Carburetor

Fuel Line

Figs. 9-5 (right) and 9-6 (below). Plumb the "double pumper" four-barrel carburetor. Run a small braided line through the stock fuel pump up the right side of the engine to the carb.

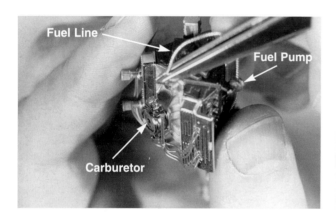

Fuel Line

Fuel Pump

Carburetor

Fig. 9-7. The completed front end of the model stock car, including the chassis, suspension, and engine compartment. Paint the dual Monroe front shocks yellow on the main cylinder and silver on the shaft. Apply a bit of flat black with a 5-0 brush to highlight the rubber seals. Paint the radiator and oil cooler core Testor's copper bottle paint.

Figs. 9-8 and 9-9. For a more correct set of headers, remove the crossover section from each manifold side. I used a pair of wire cutters to remove them.

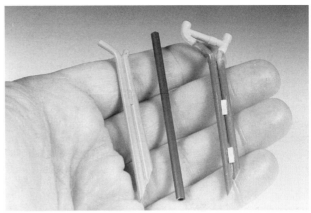

Fig. 9-10. When thoroughly dry, sand and file the puttied areas to blend into the surrounding plastic. Apply a few generous coats of primer, then lightly sand the area again. This will allow you to see if there are any rough spots that need attention. Finally, apply a final light coat of primer and then paint each set of headers the final color coat. Some headers are flat white, steel or aluminum color, or flat powder blue.

Figs. 9-11 (above) and 9-12 (below). To add a bit more realism to the side-by-side exhaust dump pipes, cut away the piece shown on the left. Use this section as a pattern and bend sections of 3/32″ plastic tubing to the same shape. Attach the new dumps into position at the end of the collectors where the original pipes were located. Some tweaking may be necessary to achieve a snug fit. The two small .020″ rectangles are used as reinforcement and represent metal plates welded to the pipes for that purpose. Next, finish the new dumps with Testor's steel paint and glue into place on the chassis.

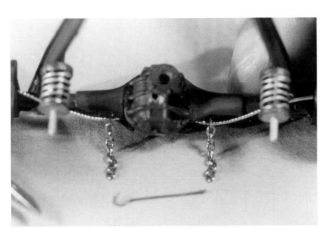

Figs. 9-13 (above left) and 9-14 (left). The rear coil springs can be detailed by first painting the recesses flat black. When they're dry, carefully detail the coils silver, yellow, red, or light blue. In most cases, race teams paint coil springs a variety of colors to represent various spring rates. Yellow is a common color.

Fig. 9-15. Stock cars use lengths of log chain to keep the rear suspension under the race car in the event of an accident. To replicate this safety device, first, cut two ⁷⁄₁₆″ lengths of jewelry chain. Make four eyelets from fine uncoated wire. Attach an eyelet to each end of the two pieces of chain. Drill two holes on either side of the differential on the top of the rear axle. Drill two corresponding holes in the cross member on the chassis above the axle. Attach the chain to the axle and then attach the other end into the holes drilled in the cross member. You can add a rear-end cooler pump made from thin sheet plastic. Attach the pump onto the back end of the drive shaft just ahead of the rear-end snout. Modern race cars use aircraft-type hoses and color-anodized fittings. I still use various diameters of silver craft braid found at my local craft store for the oil lines. Once the drive line and engine plumbing are complete, a quick way to give the appearance of aircraft fittings on various components is to use a small dab of Tamiya transparent red and blue at the junction of the line and the accessory. Paint a ¹⁄₁₆″ section of the craft braid blue where it joins the component. Repeat this with transparent red right next to the blue section.

Fig. 9-16. The finished rear suspension, including the brake lines, oil cooling lines, rear end cooling pump, and safety chains.

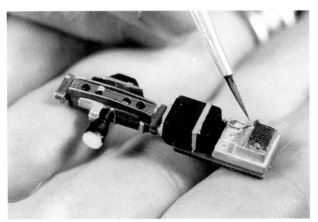

Fig. 9-17. Paint the dashboard flat black. Then detail the switch panel with aluminum paint. Paint the instrument bezels silver and carefully pick out the raised gauge face engraving with flat white bottle paint and a fine brush. Paint the gauge pointer or needle on each instrument face flat red.

Fig. 9-18. Once the roll cage is assembled and painted, use vinyl tubing like the roll cage padding produced by Scale Model Speedways. Cut the padding to length as required. Split each section of padding lengthwise (like a hot dog bun). Then gently spread the tubing open just enough to slip it onto and around the roll cage bars.

Fig. 9-19. The early in-car camera added nearly 20 extra pounds to the total weight of the race car. The Monogram kit contains a reasonable facsimile. If you choose to include it in your model, detail-paint the camera with various shades of metallic gray, aluminum, silver, and flat black for added realism.

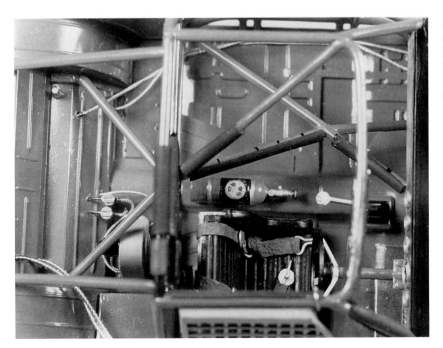

Fig. 9-20. The completed race car cockpit should look a lot like this one. Clearly seen here are the roll cage padding and driver's seat with safety belts made from ⅛"-wide strips of masking tape painted flat black.

Fig. 9-21. Conversion kits can easily turn many of the early Monogram GM stock cars into versions that were never available from the plastic kit manufacturers. The JNJ conversion kit for the '86–'87 Pontiac 2+2 is an excellent example. The new aero nose is cast in resin. Scrub this piece thoroughly with Soft Scrub or soak it for a couple of days in Wesley's Tire Cleaner to remove the mold release. Adding a mounting tab cut from sheet plastic will make attaching the new nose a great deal easier. Following the instruction sheet, cut away a portion of the rear deck with a razor saw. Trim out the vacuum-formed new rear deck section. Some filing and sanding may be necessary to achieve that final fit. Glue the vacuum-formed deck section into place. When all the conversion pieces are in place your Pontiac 2+2 should look like this on both ends. A bit of body filler may be necessary around the seams where the new rear deck section joins the injection-molded body. All the major body work is finished. Carefully trim the clear vacuum-formed rear window down to size. Work slowly and trim the rear window roughly to size, making sure not to remove too much material at one time.

Fig. 9-22. Proceed to paint, assemble, and detail your 2+2 just as you would a regular injection-molded kit. This 1986 Alugard Pontiac is painted Ford Mustang Acapulco Blue with a Testor's no. 3 red interior and chassis. The decals are from Fred Cady Design. Rusty Wallace recorded his first Winston Cup victory at Bristol, Tennessee, in 1986 in this car.

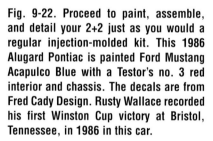

Driver figure

Fig. 9-23. The final touch for any stock car model is the addition of a driver figure. I have used two different items. Some issues of Monogram Stock Car Plus kits contained a driver figure. This figure appears to represent a male over 6 feet tall. Though I have used this figure otherwise, it is best used with race cars using the Butler seat, since space is tight in the cockpit. Replicas and Miniatures of Maryland does offer a driver figure more to the proportions of a Mark Martin or Jeff Gordon. The resin figure comes with a choice of open or full-face style helmets. Remember that human skin and most all types of clothing has a flat or semigloss finish. You can easily brush-paint your driver with helmet and uniform to complement the color scheme of his race car. Here's where good reference material comes in handy.

1991 roll cage modifications

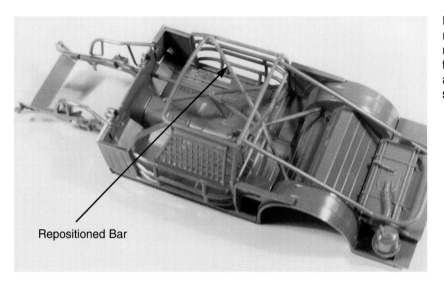

Repositioned Bar

Fig. 9-24. For the 1991 season, NASCAR mandated a change in the structure of the roll cage. This involves the simple relocation of what many call the Petty bar. This assembled chassis and roll cage represent the location of this bar prior to 1991.

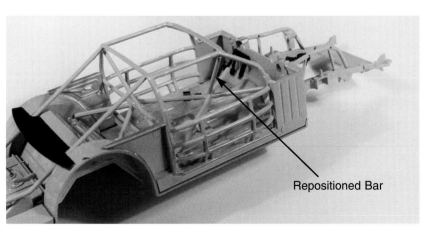

Repositioned Bar

Fig. 9-25. Since the beginning of 1991, the Petty bar has been repositioned as shown here. This simply requires trimming the length of the bar until it fits snugly into the new position.

Roof rails

Fig. 9-26. Starting in early 1988, NASCAR mandated roof rails. These are a pair of thin sheet metal ribs running parallel to the center line of the car along the top, above the side windows. Mark a line on each side of the top 1/8″ above the edge of the window openings. Use a razor saw to cut through the top surface along the line. Stop short of the window frames front and rear.

Fig. 9-27. Next, cut two strips of .010 sheet plastic 5/16″ wide and slightly longer than the cut just made. The cut a small notch in each end of the strip so it slides into the cut in the top of the body shell. Test-fit the strip into the groove cut into the top. When you are satisfied with the fit, glue each strip into place. Use a sanding block or tool to shape the rails to their final form. The roof rails should be about 3/32″ tall when finished.

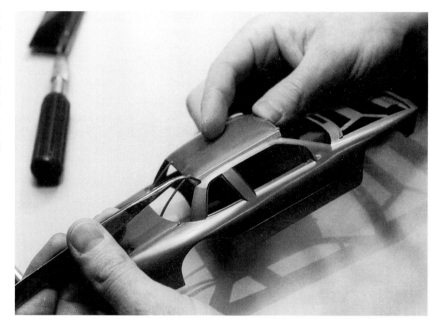

10

BOX STOCKERS

BUILDING AND DETAILING A MONOGRAM 1994 LUMINA OUT-OF-THE-BOX

Len Carsner built this replica of Sterling Marlin's Daytona 500–winning '94 Chevy Lumina. Whether you build OTB or curbside, you can add loads of detail to separate your model from the field.

For the 1988 NASCAR Winston Cup season, Buick, Oldsmobile, and Pontiac introduced the new General Motors "W" body shell. This represented the first time the sanctioning body allowed the use of body styles not manufactured as rear-drive, street-driven cars. The new automotive shapes were hung on the standard NASCAR 110-inch-wheelbase V-8 powered chassis, even though none could be dealer-ordered with anything but a push-rod V-6 engine. The new GM race cars were commonly referred to as "silhouette race cars."

The Ford Thunderbird, redesigned for the 1989 season, remained a rear-drive production car. For 1988, the Chevrolet teams were left to continue on with the aged Monte Carlo SS, even though production had ceased with the 1987 model year.

Chevrolet's new W-based production car was delayed a year. That GM division was hard at work on an MC replacement to be called Lumina. This too was a front-drive, street-driven car and would take the same form as its sister divisions on the way to the race track.

The production Chevrolet Lumina two-door coupe was many months late to market. But six months early, NASCAR allowed Chevrolet race teams to use the new sheet metal for the spring race at Talledega. In its racing debut, Dale Earnhardt rode the racing rear-drive V-8 powered Lumina to what seemed, at the time, an easy victory.

Chevrolet reskinned the Lumina two-door for 1995 and reintroduced the Monte Carlo nameplate for the car. Odd, since Chevrolet had enjoyed phenomenal success with the Lumina,

capturing the title in 1990, 1991, 1993, and again in 1994. Chevrolet followed this domination by taking the driver's and manufacturer's titles in 1995 and 1996 with the newly reintroduced Monte Carlo.

Emerging from relative obscurity for the 1990 season, the Morgan-McClure team joined forces with a young Ernie Irvan to campaign the Kodak-sponsored Chevrolet. Success came quickly with the team's and driver's first pole and first WC victory at the spring race at Bristol, Tennessee. The Kodak team with Ernie behind the wheel was suddenly very competitive, winning the 1991 Daytona 500.

Sterling Marlin replaced Irvan in the Kodak race car at the end of the 1993 season. The winning tradition continued as Marlin won the 1994 and 1995 Daytona 500s back to back.

Leonard Carsner shows us how to

build a contest-quality box-stock Lumina based on the Monogram Kellogg's no. 5 kit. There are at least three variations on the Monogram Lumina kit, representing the race car through various stages of its development and reflecting the ever-changing rule book.

Out-of-the-box model building is a worthy effort recognized in virtually all competitive model contests today. This category restricts the use of exotic detailing materials and advanced building techniques in favor of a more level playing field. Basic building skills get all the attention here, rewarding the modeler who chooses a building subject wisely and executes fit, finish, painting techniques, and small details well.

Getting started

There's no substitute for plenty of accurate reference materials. Pit Pass features from *Scale Auto Enthusiast*

magazine and race reports from *Circle Track* magazine are a good resource. Detail Master offers a twelve-page color booklet, *Vantage Point,* chronicling the 1994 Kodak Lumina virtually down to the last nut and bolt. Fortunately, newsstands today are loaded with full-color publications brimming with valuable detailing information for the scale modeler.

Paint, tools, etc.

Virtually everything needed for an OTB or curbside project is as close as your nearest hobby shop. Testor's produces tools, adhesives, and dozens of colors and shades of spray and bottle paint to help replicate your favorite stock car model.

BSR Replicas and Finishes sells automotive primers and primary paint colors exactly like the colors used on the Kodak Chevrolets. With some experimentation you may find other paints and primers that will work well

on the interior, roll cage, and chassis components.

Realistic Racing Colors offers a full line of NASCAR-correct race car paint colors in both spray can and bottle. Aftermarket decals, aftermarket tampo-printed tires or dry-transfer sidewall marking all fall within the spirit of OTB rules.

Building the kit

Monogram's Kellogg's Chevrolet no. 5 Lumina kit is the proper choice to replicate an accurate box-stock '94 Kodak Chevy stock car. Protect clear and plated parts until they're needed by wrapping the trees in see-through Glad Wrap.

Close examination of the chassis reveals many ejector pin marks (little circular impressions in the plastic) that you'll have to remove by filing and sanding until smooth. Also remove the company logo and copyright date molded into the chassis surface.

Figs. 10-2 and 10-3. Two views of the front and rear of the three variations of Monogram Chevrolet Lumina. From left to right: '89–'92, '93, and 1994. Note the differences in the front spoilers and rear bumpers.

Painting

Fig. 10-4. Brush-paint the inside surfaces of the body flat black once the exterior color is dry. The patch on the inside surface is flat red and represents the insulated pad on the actual race car.

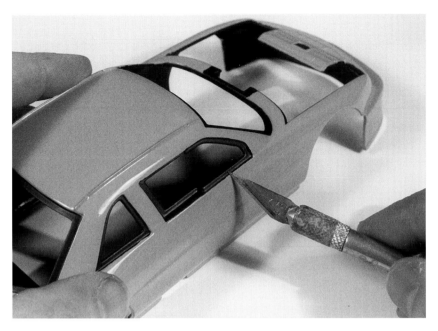

Fig. 10-5. Paint the recessed surrounds with Testor's Black Chrome bottle paint applied with a fine brush. To clean up the edges, use a fresh X-Acto blade and a steady hand. Scrape gently, using very little pressure. After the primary body color is thoroughly dry, give the finish an even higher gloss by using a polishing kit. Use the finer grades of sandpaper, like 4000, 6000, 8000, and 12000 grit first, and then wrap it up with white polish and a soft cloth. Never use wax on a model race car body shell until all the graphics have been put in place. Many times water-slide decals do not stick well to waxed surfaces.

Applying decals and cleaning up

Double- and triple-check the alignment of each decal to make sure it's situated properly while it can still be moved (before it dries completely). Once all the decals have had time to dry sufficiently, gently wipe the whole body with a damp facial tissue. Finally, there are three liquids that can be very handy when completing your box-stock race car. Fantastik is great for cleaning the residue, water marks, and fingerprints from the body surfaces after all the decals are in place. Kodak Film Cleaner on a cotton swab is great for cleaning the clear parts once they are attached in place in the body shell, especially if you've used a white, water-based glue. Pledge household furniture wax works well over paint and decals as the final touch for your model.

Under the skin

Fig. 10-6. Since the interior, roll cage, front snout, and front and rear suspension components are all gloss black on the Kodak Lumina, painting these parts is pretty easy. However, this means that detail-painting—using 3-0 and 5-0 brushes and a steady hand to apply a variety of metallic colors—is vitally important. Time to check out that all-important reference material for the minute details!

Fig. 10-7. Since the kit plastic is light in color, paint each coil spring flat black, then carefully file away the paint to reveal the contrasting color.

Fig. 10-8. Note the surface areas painted silver on these suspension contact points. Remove a small bit of material from the coil springs to reduce the ride height of your model.

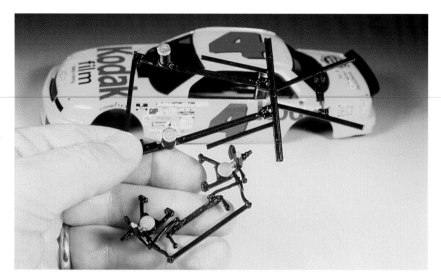

Fig. 10-9. Use Testor's Metalizers along with other standard Testor's bottle paints to give that realistic final look to the engine and its accessory components like the belt pulleys and exhaust dumps. Follow closely the information presented in the Detail Master Vantage Point booklet. Liberal use of Testor's black, aluminum, silver, and various Metalizer colors makes for a realistic engine and race car suspension pieces.

Fig. 10-10. Paint the Butler-built driver's seat flat black first. Then use a five-point safety harness decal from a Blue Ridge sheet to provide a realistic-looking unit. Just trim it out like any other decal, soak it in water, and slide it into place.

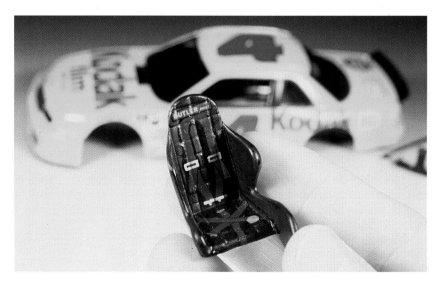

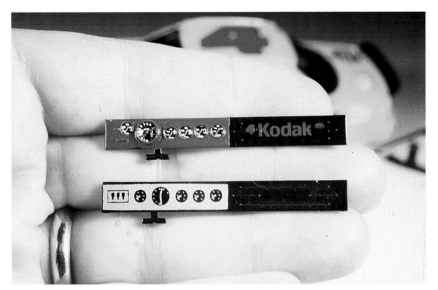

Fig. 10-11. You have a couple of options for detailing the dash. To duplicate the one on top, first paint the dash red. Apply individual water-slide decal faces to each instrument housing and corporate logos on the passenger side. To duplicate the one at the bottom, sand and file off the molded-in instrument details. Paint the dash flat black, then apply a gauge panel decal.

Fig. 10-12. Cover the shaded area of the front and rear glass, using flat black bottle paint applied from the inside. Another option is to use Chartpak black tape over these areas.

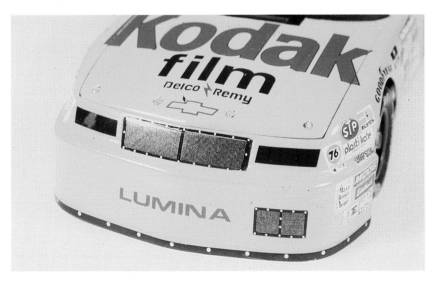

Fig. 10-13. Using aftermarket water-slide decals for grille mesh and cooling vent hardware makes this Kodak Lumina look like the real thing.

Fig. 10-14. Accurate and skillful use of metallic shades of Testor's bottle paints contrasted against the stark black chassis is a real attention-getter.

Fig. 10-15. It's pretty simple to put that little red line around the edge of the rim on your stock car wheels. First spray a light coat of red paint on a few square inches of smooth cardboard. Next press each open side down squarely into the fresh paint. Just that quick, your Bassett stock car wheel will have that distinctive red line around the outside edge. Adding the red line to this Bassett wheel along with the other tire and wheel details makes for a very realistic-looking combination.

Fig. 10-16. This Interstate Batteries Monte Carlo built by Mike Madlinger would be an excellent choice for either a box-stock or curbside project. Note the additional engine plumbing details that Monogram has added to the Monte Carlo kit compared to the Lumina (fig. 10-9).

Fig. 10-17. Curbside or box-stock competition permits the addition of such details as the simulated electrical tape Mike Madlinger added here to the hood pins used on race cars during qualifying.

Fig. 10-18. The curbside contest class permits the builder to add a lot more details. Here, Mike Madlinger has added an aircraft-type fuel filler and overflow pipe from Race Ready Replicas.

11
HIGH-TECH T

BUILDING AND DETAILING A CONTEST-WINNING NASCAR THUNDERBIRD

Tom Anderson's Family Channel Thunderbird. Drop this model in front of a scene of typical pit road activities, and you would probably not be able to distinguish it from the full-size version. Is there any accessory or detail missing under the hood? Unless you're a NASCAR crew chief or at least a race car technician, then only Tom knows for sure! He scribed open the trunk lid and hinged it using photoetched pieces from Oval Track Hobbies. Tom patiently researched every part, piece, and detail of the full-size stock car engine compartment and painstakingly replicated it item for item. He discarded the kit front hoop and replaced it entirely by a scratchbuilt unit formed from solder wire. Pat Covert photo.

Fig. 11-2. Tom started with the time-honored Monogram chassis replicating a Banjo Matthews classic rear-steer unit. This underside view shows the hand-crafted exhaust system, elaborate body panel bracing, and every hose and cable. Even the smallest bolt heads are represented by photoetched pieces. Pat Covert photo.

Fig. 11-3. Not only does Tom Anderson throw "everything but the kitchen sink" at a Monogram T-Bird, but this Dupont Lumina driven by Jeff Gordon is testament that his modeling skills are nonpartisan. Pat Covert photo.

NASCAR stock car racing finally arrived in the '90s. Every event drew capacity crowds, many new multimillion dollar race tracks were built, and television ratings put stock car racing on a par with football, basketball, and baseball. Corporate America engaged in the sport of outbidding one another for the right to spend millions to display their product name on the flank of a stock car. Some sponsors even settled for a tiny spot on the deck lid! Stock car racing became the topic of conversation around the office water cooler. Drivers like Earnhardt, Gordon, Labonte, Jarrett, Wallace, and Elliott became household names.

The NASCAR stock car continued to evolve slowly into a sophisticated relic. The parts, pieces, and equipment were state-of-the-art. Basic technol-ogy, simply put, made it a gilded antique. For the modern stock car, underpinnings of the '90s had changed very little from the original Holman-Moody 1965 Ford Galaxies. The '90s stock-based race car still used a push rod V-8 with a four-barrel carburetor. The driveline was still rear-wheel drive utilizing a nearly bullet-proof Ford 9-inch differential, though most pas-senger cars were front-wheel drive V-6s. The stock car racing four-speed manual transmission owed a great deal of its heritage to the Borg-Warner T-10 used in Dodge and Plymouth muscle cars of the late '60s.

Compared to NASCAR stockers of just a decade ago, current examples are loaded with sophisticated electron-ics, miniature TV cameras aimed at the bumper, cockpit, suspension, and dri-ver, aircraft-style plumbing, pumps, and coolers, and NASA-style driver's cool suits. Individually hand-crafted seats, chassis, suspension components, and body shells are combined with the latest tire and brake system technology. The modern NASCAR stocker is both an enigma and a paradox. Why . . . just the term "stock car" is at the very least an oxymoron!

Building scale replicas of the NASCAR stock cars remains a staple of the automotive modeling hobby. Sales of plastic stock car kits, now in the millions, continue to spawn an ever-growing aftermarket industry that supplies everything short of scale gas fumes and tire smoke!

Tom Anderson is among a select few model car builders engaged in an all-out campaign to create the most complete and in-depth likeness of the contemporary NASCAR stock car in

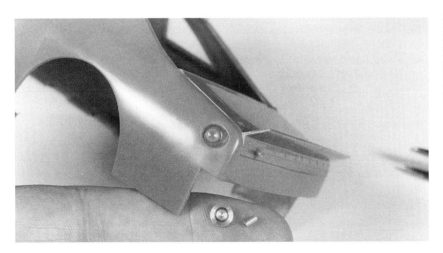

Fig. 11-4. The aircraft-style dry break fuel inlet kit from Race Ready Replicas includes an overflow tube as well. Tom re-moved just a small portion of the molded-in filler neck, and the machined fuel inlet dropped right into place.

Figs. 11-5 and 11-6. Tom molded in the front spoiler and removed the complete kit grille. He filled all seams with Dr. Micro Tools body filler. He added a ⅛"-wide strip of .010 sheet plastic to the lower edge of the kit spoiler. This formed a platform in preparation for installing a Model Car Garage photoetched front air dam as part of the final assembly. The surface detail is excellent, especially the many pop rivets.

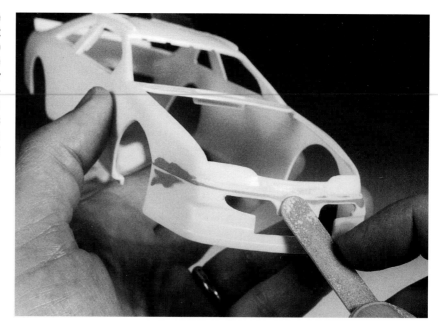

miniature each time he produces something. The Family Channel T-Bird seen here is the result of 450 to 500 hours of intense work over a ten-month period that, as he says, "requires gobs of research, fervent endurance, and above all unlimited patience."

At the top of Tom's list of absolute necessities for building a model like this one is Race Fan's Reference: *Understanding Winston Cup Racing,* by William M. Burt. Anderson found this full-color softbound book to be the best source for information about the current stock car technology, literally down to the last pop rivet.

Of course, there are many other excellent publications on the subject of stock cars, like *The Anatomy & Development of the Stock Car,* by Dr. John Craft, *Winston Cup Illustrated, Circle Track,* and *Stock Car Racing* magazines, and the occasional Pit Pass feature in *Scale Auto Enthusiast.*

To tell the whole story of the building and detailing of Tom Anderson's 'Bird would fill an entire book. We will describe briefly much of what you see here. And in addition, Tom will explain selected tips and techniques in depth.

The body and chassis

Anderson started with a Monogram 1994 NASCAR Thunderbird 1/24 scale kit. He created functional roof flaps from sheet aluminum (figs. 11-7, 11-8, and 11-9). Tom scribed open the trunk lid and hinged it along with the hood, using Oval Track Hobbies photoetched hinge mechanisms. Then he used thin sheet aluminum to scratchbuild various items, including the cowl air intake, the radiator shroud (fig. 11-12), the crush panels on the firewall, the interior mounting panels, the fuel cell, and many small panels on the underside of the chassis. Tom scribed the outline for cowl flaps into the panel at the base of the windshield. Since current rules dictate a much larger unit than on the kit,

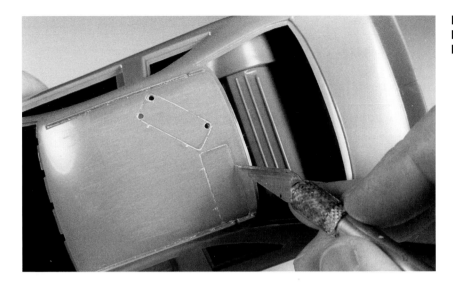

Fig. 11-7. The engraved kit roof flaps can be scribed out or removed by first drilling holes in all four corners.

Fig. 11-9. Here an assembled roof flap has been constructed using the diagram provided. Each roof flap fits into the opening in the roof panel. Tom bent the ends of each wire hinge at 90 degrees, then inserted it into one of the two sets of small diameter holes. He drilled two holes just 1/32″ apart originally in case the hinge needed some adjustment.

Fig. 11-8. Working from the inside of the body shell, Tom used a jeweler's file to clean up the new opening for the articulated roof flaps. It is very important that both openings be perfectly square to ensure that the flaps will operate properly. Note also the 1/32″ x 3/32″ slots cut into the front edge of the flap openings 3/16″ from either end. He also drilled a pair of .030″ holes alongside the slots 1/16″ from either end.

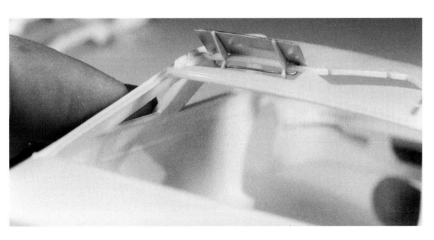

Fig. 11-10. Tom adjusted the hinge until the flap moved smoothly as well as opening and closing completely. He applied a minute dab of Vaseline with a toothpick inside to each hinge bracket where it made contact with the wire. This eliminated primer and paint buildup on these delicate parts. The Vaseline was easy to wipe away during final assembly.

Fig. 11-11. Left to right, the kit chassis, kit radiator, and Tom's handformed shroud. Tom used .006 printer's shim material for the shroud, but you could also use machinist's shim stock.

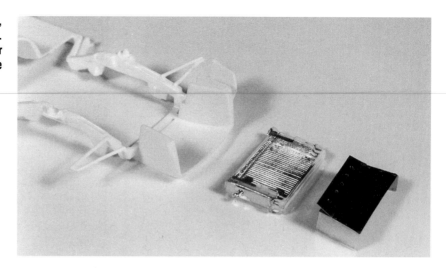

Fig. 11-12. The chassis is displayed right side up with the kit radiator and new hand-formed shroud installed. Tom used .006 printer's shim material for the shroud. Also recommended for forming such a delicate part is machinist's shim stock.

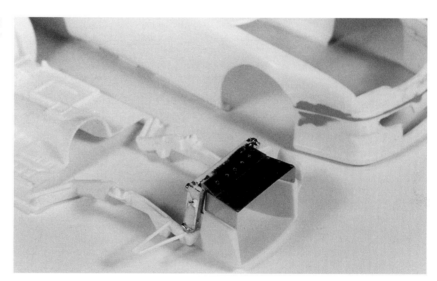

Fig. 11-13. Tom used bicycle handlebar grip material to replicate the half-round roll cage padding commonly used on NASCAR stockers of the '90s. First he cut a section about two inches square from the material. Then Tom carefully sliced tissue-thin sheets of the grip material with a razor blade. Extreme caution must be used when working with a razor blade. Here is an interior and exterior view of the grip material attached to the roll cage. Use super glue to keep this stuff in place.

Fig. 11-14. On the left is the top portion of the kit fuel cell in place. On the right is the base platform Tom made for his fuel cell from .010 sheet aluminum. The dimensions are 1½″ x 1¹/₁₆″. The pop rivets are photoetched pieces.

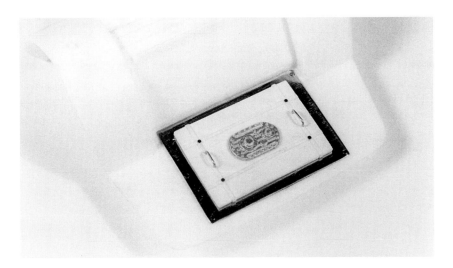

Figs. 11-15 and 11-16. Tom detailed an ABC Resin fuel cell by adding the photoetched platform, top center, the lifting handles made from .030 wire, and four photoetched pop rivets. The fuel cell is now ready for installation of the filler neck and overflow tube.

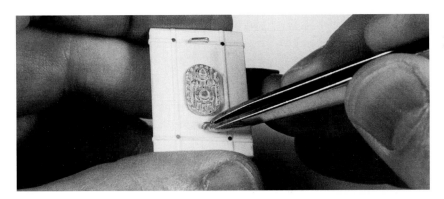

he scratchbuilt the rear spoiler. Front and rear panels were molded in; he cut out the kit grille work and replaced it with OTH's photoetched grille sections along with Scale Scenics' brass micromesh screen (figs. 11-5, 11-6). Tom added left and right side aerodynamic skirts along with a modified front air dam. Final detailing included operating photoetched hood and deck lid pins and a machined aircraft dry-break fuel inlet from Race Ready Replicas (fig. 11-4).

Tom used most of the chassis and suspension pieces from the kit except the front hoop. For this he used .060 plastic rod to hand-form an updated unit. He scratchbuilt the shock absorbers and shock towers and made the brake cooling ducts by wrapping wire around tubing and covering it with Bare-Metal foil. Tom hand-formed the exhaust dumps from aluminum tubing and drilled them out to accommodate cooling tubes.

The interior

Next, Tom flocked the kit seat to resemble a fabric finish and covered the back panel with Bare-Metal matte-finish foil to give the appearance of an aluminum frame. He then added a pre-assembled aftermarket five-point harness to the seat. Roll bar padding was formed from a bicycle handlebar grip. Detail Resources photoetched stock car detailing kit provided the interior window braces and fire extinguisher. Tom scratchbuilt the shifter handle and dashboard from plastic sheet and bar stock. The instruments actually are lighted using miniature LEDs powered by hearing-aid batteries hidden in the fuel cell in the trunk. The oil reservoir

fan housing, two-way radio, rear-end fluid reservoir, and interior cooling ducts were scratchbuilt.

Inside the trunk

Tom scratchbuilt the fuel cell platform from sheet aluminum and made the handles from .030 wire along with various items like the clear fuel tube from the Detail Resources kit.

The engine

The basic kit block/transmission, cylinder heads, and intake manifold were used with a photoetched belt and pulley set from Model Car Garage. The carb is a resin piece from Pro-Tech, the prewired distributor is from Scale Repro, and the oil breathers, aircraft hose fittings, braided oil lines, electric fans, and NASCAR-style air cleaner are from Detail Master. Tom used a Trae and Dad MSD ignition box and Performance Detail Products Accel Super Coil. Carb fittings and linkages

are photoetched pieces from Detail Master, the throttle return spring is made by Trae and Dad, and the oil filter is made by Curbside Dioramas. Anderson scratchbuilt the filter diaphragm. He hand-made the radiator shroud from .010 aluminum sheet and hand-formed the exhaust headers from .062 solid-core solder wire.

The wheels and tires

Tom used a set of resin nine-hole wheels made by ABC Resin. The center spindle hole and the five lug hole are predrilled (figs. 11-17, 11-18, and 11-19). Tom carefully sliced eight Monogram kit tires down the middle (bagel-style) at a 40/60 split. Then he bonded the larger halves back together to form a "beefier," slightly more aggressive-looking race car tire. Kit-based or various after-market side wall markings are available, either dry-transfer or water-slide (fig. 11-22). Tom used an Ertl-AMT decal for the

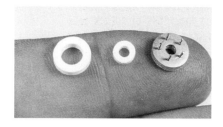

Fig. 11-17. From left to right: a 1/16″ piece of 5/16″ tubing, a 1/16″ piece of 3/16″ tubing, and a finished five-lug hub. The smaller doughnut fits inside the larger ring.

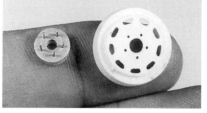

Figs. 11-18 and 11-19. Next, Tom placed the new hub on the back of an ABC Resin five-lug wheel and lined it up with the center hole. Then he used the predrilled lug stud holes as a guide to drill the five corresponding holes in the hub.

Fig. 11-20. On the right is the Monogram T-Bird kit carburetor. On the left is a Pro-Tech resin four-barrel carb. Tom cut four 3/32″ lengths of 1/16″ tubing and inserted them into the four holes to represent the throats or venturi.

Fig. 11-21. Tom kept the small lengths of aluminum tubing attached to a piece of tape until he could glue them into place in the carb.

Fig. 11-22. There are many aftermarket products to reproduce the yellow Goodyear sidewall lettering, including dry-transfer and water-slide decals. The Gofer Racing Goodyear Dry Transfers are easy to use by simply rubbing them onto the tire sidewall. However, make sure the surface is free of dirt and grease, and be sure to line up the lettering properly. Also make sure to burnish the lettering thoroughly before removing the transfer sheet from the tire surface.

Fig. 11-23. NASCAR issues this memo to race teams dictating contingency sponsor decal placement on the right and left front fenders of each race car. Depending on where you finish and whose sticker is on your race car, those contingency decals can be worth thousands of dollars to a team each season. Slixx and JNJ produce contingency decal sheets. Some sheets have them grouped in a cluster and others have them free-standing. Many stock car kit decal sheets also have appropriate sponsor decals.

yellow lettering. Anderson used valve stems made by Pro-Tech, and the lug nuts are no. 1 adapter fittings from Detail Master. For the 20 lug nut studs, Tom cut short lengths of LMG 0000-160 threaded rod and then inserted them into holes in the hubs. This allows for the wheels to actually be bolted on the model and unbolted, just like the full-size race car.

The paint

Tom primed the major components with Plasti-cote white primer. He then painted the body shell and interior Boyd's bright white. The second body color is BSR's Electric Blue acrylic enamel. Tom painted the underside of the chassis Testor's Gunship Gray and finally used Boyd's red paint on the spoiler and roof rails.

Anderson painted the model over a two-week period to allow sufficient drying time for each coat of paint. He rubbed out each color coat and gave it a high polish with an LMG Polishing Kit.

Finally, Tom applied various colors of Testor's Metalizer paint and other Testor's metallic finishes wherever necessary and drybrushed or rubbed to achieve the full effect of a metallic finish.

The graphics

Anderson used six sheets of Slixx decal no. 1077/9516 for the Family Channel Thunderbird. Not only was he seeking the most perfect printing and registration but the complexity of the decal scheme dictated the use of various pieces from multiple sheets to ensure the proper fit and placement around critical area like the operating roof flaps and the rear panels.

Other scratchbuilt items include coil springs, rear wedge adjusters, driveshaft, and engine framing. The floor jack was completely scratchbuilt from .015 sheet aluminum.

12
COLOR GALLERY

Model by Tom Anderson; Pat Covert photo.

Model by Tom Anderson; Pat Covert photo.

1940 Ford. Model by John Wise; Bill Coulter photo.

1940 Ford. Model by John Wise; Bill Coulter photo.